Textile Dyeing

THE STEP-BY-STEP GUIDE AND SHOWCASE

Kate Broughton

ROCKPORT

Acknowledgments

Special thanks to Laura Campbell, Lucinda Cathcart, Judith Content, Arnelle Dow, David and Linda France Hartge, Peggy Russell, and Carter Smith for graciously sharing their artistic tricks of the trade and for performing the step-by-step techniques shown here. Very special thanks to Don Weiner and Ellin Noble of Pro-Chemical and Dye Co. Fall River, MA, for technical review of the manuscript, for the recipes included in Chapter 8, and for the superb instruction imparted in their dye chemistry seminar.

First published in the United Stated of America by:
Rockport Publishers, Inc.
33 Commercial Street
Gloucester, Massachusetts 01930-5089
Telephone: (978) 282-9590
Fax: (978) 283-2742
www.rockpub.com

ISBN 1-56496-839-1
10 9 8 7 6 5 4 3 2

Cover Design: Francesco Jost
Layout: Laura P. Herrmann

Printed in China.

Table of Contents

Art of Light

PEGGY RUSSELL/IRO DESIGN

Introduction

Since earliest times, man has attempted to capture the colors of nature and use them for personal adornment. Prior to the invention of textiles, berries and clay, bark and roots were crushed and smeared on the body in primitive designs that evoked the primal elements of earth, water, fire, and air. When it was discovered that plants and pelts could be harvested and woven into material (anthropologists suggest it was as early as 10,000 years ago), the same colorants that were used to paint faces, vessels, and tools were employed to decorate fabric.

As with many discoveries made by early man, it was most likely by accident that various dyeing processes were stumbled upon. Over time, accident gave way to art. Different techniques —tying, binding, stamping, waxing—and different media— bleaches, pigments, beeswax, and bean paste—were developed so that multiple colors and repeating motifs could be added to the fabric. Although the designs produced by individual cultures possessed unique signatures, all were really variations on a few basic themes.

Textile dyeing has always been an art form in the Orient and so-called developing countries, but until the Industrial Revolution, it was not much of a priority in Western culture. Not until the refinement of dye chemistry in the late eighteenth century did Europeans and Americans realize that the actual coloration process was just as important to textile ornamentation as the weave.

Today, with the renewed value consumers are placing on hand-crafted objects, there has been a virtual renaissance in the art of surface design, and it seems that everyone with a creative urge is using textile dyeing as a way to express it. Fashion designers, quilters, weavers, and interior designers are satisfying their customers' demand for unique fabrications by dipping, spritzing, splashing, or soaking material in a new generation of dyes that possesses a transparent brilliance unseen two hundred years ago. Fine artists are trading in their easels and canvas and are painting on silk instead. Museums are commissioning dyers to create banners to hang from their rafters. The explosion of color and texture is as exuberant and powerful as the outpouring from a volcano.

This book is a celebration of that explosion. It presents a step-by-step guide for creating dyed fabrics using eight fundamental techniques, and features the work being produced by some of the world's most accomplished textile artists, from Carter Smith's intricately tied and discharged pieces, to David and Linda France Hartge's fabulous representational painted silks, to Arnelle Dow's multi-layered *batik* wall hangings. Many of the artists whose work is shown here—Ana Lisa Hedstrom, Judith Bird, Noel Dyrenforth—are well known in the surface design world; others are newcomers just beginning to leave their mark.

As you will see in the pages ahead, the end products of contemporary textile dyers are fresh, new, and daring, but dyeing itself remains a primal and mystical process. It is the ideal way for any artist—from novice to professional—to experience anew the wonder that came when our ancient forebears crushed those first red berries and discovered a world of infinitely colorful possibilities.

CHAPTER *1*

Textile Dyes: A Primer

LUCINDA CATHCART'S STUDIO

For almost a millennium, all dyes—with the exception of a few colors such as "antimony orange" and "manganese brown"—originated from vegetable or animal sources. Roots, berries, flower blossoms, insects, and crustacean shells were combined with minerals called mordants to yield colors that ranged from deep violet to bright yellow. No organic source was considered too off-beat if it produced a satisfactory color. A highly prized shade of scarlet, for example, was derived from the dried bodies of pregnant lice that lived on the leaves of Mediterranean evergreen shrubs. The color was so popular that, in 1464, Pope Paul II decreed that it be used to dye the robes of Catholic cardinals!

Dyeing was such a complex art in the Middle Ages that workers were sub-divided into different guilds—"black dyers," "dyers of high colors," and "silk dyers". Part alchemy, part art, the production of dyestuffs remained unchanged until 1856. British student William Henry Perkin inadvertently created the first synthetic dyestuff when his attempt to synthesize quinine resulted in a brilliant purple stain. He quickly obtained a patent, quit school, and marketed the dye commercially. From that time on, a steady stream of colors, and new ways to marry them to fabric, has flooded the world of textiles.

Although dye chemistry has changed, the process of dyeing continues to be both a science and an art. Once you have a fundamental understanding of what it is you are using, and why and how it works, your only limitation is your imagination.

Living Color

If you are not already familiar with textile dyes, you will soon discover that there are many types and many brands available. This diversity can be very confusing, especially once you realize that different names are often used for the same type of dye.

The discussion that follows is meant to give you a quick overview of the dye market and to familiarize you with the buzzwords and terminology you will encounter. Because instructions for use vary from dealer to dealer and brand to brand, we have refrained from providing specific measures for any techniques illustrated on the following pages. For more precise information, we strongly suggest that you establish a good working relationship with your nearest supplier (see Appendix for resources). The customer-service representatives for each company will help you select the right type of dye for your project and will send you detailed instruction sheets.

Finally, keep an open mind, build up a stock of catalogs to compare merchandise, and familiarize yourself with different brand names. Be willing to compare and experiment, and remember that many artists have preferences based on their personal idiosyncrasies rather than scientific principles.

There are ten classifications of dyes that can be used to color fabric: azoic, basic, disperse, mordant, pigment, sulfur, vat, direct, acid, and reactive. Because they are easy to use, the last three types—direct, acid, and fiber-reactive—are most often used by artists, crafters, and teachers.

Direct Dyes

These dyes are widely available, and are sold in relatively mainstream places such as supermarkets and convenience stores. Available in powdered or liquid form (popular brands include *RIT*® and *Tintex*®), direct dyes are economical and easy to use (for example, they do not need to be set with steam or a timed, temperature-controlled bath).

Generally speaking, however, the wash-fastness of direct dyes is not as good as that of acid and fiber-reactive dyes, and they lack a certain brilliance. As you will see in the pages that follow, none of the artists featured favor direct dyes for their projects.

Acid Dyes

The name sounds foreboding, but acid dyes are not themselves acids. Their name is derived from the fact that they need to be mixed with salt and an acidic medium such as vinegar, ammonium sulfate, or citric acid in order to bond to the fabric. Because they are particularly recommended for use with wool and silk, some dye suppliers call this class of colorants "protein dyes." Although there are three classes of acid dyes, Class III—also known as "hot-water," "weak," or "milling" dyes—is the one textile artists generally come in contact with. Class III dyes require less acid and less salt than Class I and II dyes, and possess excellent wash- and light-fastness.

Acid dyes are often called hot-water dyes because in order for the color to mate and set with the fabric, the dye bath must be brought to a specified temperature (the manufacturer will indicate the appropriate range) and kept there for a specified length of time. Typically, the dye bath is warmed to moderate heat (150°F/65.5°C to 185°F/85°C) for 15 minutes and gently stirred, then raised again to 210°F/98°C and kept there for an hour. (Silk should remain at 185°F/85°C to protect the serecin coating on the fiber.) You can leave the material in the dye bath for a shorter length of time, but the intensity of color will be less. As an alternative to a dye bath, acid dyes can also be applied directly from a room-temperature solution and then steamed. For this reason, acid dyes are also some-times referred to as steam-set dyes.

When the proper amount of time has elapsed and the fabric is removed, the water in which the acid dye was mixed will be almost completely clear. This is because the color was pulled, or "exhausted," out of the water and into the fiber. If the color doesn't exhaust, it is your tip-off that the dyeing process did not take hold.

Fiber-Reactive Dyes

These dyes bond to the fiber in a unique molecular process that ensures light-fastness, wash-fastness, and brilliant color. They are favored for use on cellulose fibers such as cotton, linen, and rayon, but also work exceptionally well on silk.

There are four groups of fiber-reactive dyes: very highly reactive, highly reactive, moderately reactive, and slightly reactive. The term *reactivity* refers to how quickly the color bonds with the fabric at room temperature. Reactive dyes are very sensitive to time and temperature. If not allowed to "steep" or cure on the fabric for the allotted number of minutes or hours, the dye will be adsorbed rather than absorbed; this means the color will merely sit on the surface of the fiber and will eventually rub off.

Natural Dyes

Very highly reactive dyes are the most popular and easy to use of the four groups. They are often referred to as cold-water dyes, but this is a misnomer; no dyes will set in truly cold water. Dyes in this group can, however, set at room temperature (the room must be above 70°F/22°C), which makes them exceptionally well-suited for direct application of multiple colors—a painter's dream! Brand names you will encounter in this category include Procion MX and Sumifix.

Slightly reactive dyes require steam to activate the chemical process. However, they cannot be surpassed for their depth and clarity of color, and are favored by many professional artists for that reason. The Procion H series of dyes belongs to this category.

There are several recommended methods for using reactive dyes. In general, the options range from air-curing for a full 24 hours; allowing the fabric to air-dry for a specific length of time, followed by curing in a steamer or hot-hot-hot clothes dryer; or variations on these two themes.

Is natural better? Many artists have expressed a desire to get back to basics and to use natural dyes—roots, berries, and barks—in the belief that they are somehow safer and less caustic. This belief is misguided. Although experimenting with natural dyestuffs for historic purposes or for the pure challenge is certainly worth doing, there are many reasons for the average artist and craftsperson to stay away from them:

• **Natural dyes do not have coloring power in themselves.** They have to be used with a mordant— usually some kind of metallic salt—in order for the dye to be imparted onto the fiber. Many of these metals are suspected carcinogens.

• **The materials themselves are quite costly.**

• **It is very difficult to achieve accurate color matching when working with natural dyes.**

• **Natural dyes tend not to have good wash-fastness.** Indigo, in particular, is notorious for bleeding. (Not bad if you're a madras manufacturer; disastrous if you're dyeing a hank of wool for a child's sweater!)

Pigments

In the last decade, numerous new products have come on the market that allow artists to add color, pattern, and texture to fabric. The most versatile of these are the pigments—often interchangeably referred to as "fabric paints." Pigments generally are easy to use, don't require the surface preparation that dyeing does, and generally require little or no heating or fixing. However, they differ from dyes in significant ways:

• *Dyes bond with the fiber and penetrate it; pigments sit on the surface of the fabric.* Although pigments can soak into the fabric to create the illusion of having permeated the fiber, no chemical process has taken place to fuse the coloring chemicals into the molecules of the fiber. Over time a pigment can and will rub off. This is why pigment-colored garments often have a hang-tag recommending that they be turned inside-out before laundering.

• *Dyes are transparent; pigments are opaque.* If you immerse a floral printed fabric with a white background into a tub of blue dye, the flowers will not be obscured; the background will be blue and the flowers will have a bluish tint that blends with their previous color. If you apply a blue pigment to a floral fabric, however, the pigment will completely obscure the design.

• *Pigments tend to make fabric stiff; dyes do not affect the "hand" of the material.* (This is changing, however. A new generation of improved pigments for silk painting and other surface ornamentation have recently come onto the market and render surprising results. Ask your supplier about items such as *Pebeo SetaSilk* and *SetaColor,* and *Deka PermAir* and *Deka Permanent.*)

For the most part, this book will focus on coloring fabric with dyes. Because of the popularity of marbling, however, we have also included a chapter on this technique even though pigments are used more often than dyes to create the marvelous feathered and dappled look we associate with marbled materials.

ARNELLE DOW
Dye Shelf

CHAPTER 2

Techniques & Tools

SALLY JONES
Fabric silk-screened with fiber-reactive dyes

Although novices and mathematically minded artists yearn for formulas and rules, most experienced dyers warn against getting too hung up on the "thou shalt" approach. In spite of their intimate knowledge of the medium, all of the artists who contributed to this book admit that the magical, unexpected results that come from letting happenstance take over are the true rewards of working with dyes. Carter Smith, one of the most accomplished textile artists working today, adamantly stresses the importance of avoiding preoccupation with strict formulas. "Let dyeing take you where it will," he says. "Otherwise what you're doing is science, not art."

Precision does have its place: A working knowledge of dye mixology and attention to precise measuring makes for a safer work environment and helps prevent waste. Beyond these concerns, however, your need for precision depends upon how badly you want to get controlled, repeatable results. If you are producing a custom-designed upholstery fabric for a client, this may be important. If you are producing one-of-a-kind hand-painted garments, predictability may be the last thing you want.

Regardless of your goals or needs, the tips that follow are important to consider as you outfit your work space.

Safety First

Dyes are chemicals and should be treated as such. Vapors, mists, and dust—a few of the by-products of working with dyes—can be inhaled as you work; or ingested if you consume food left uncovered in your work space. Therefore do not underestimate the importance of following these safety measures:

🍒 Tip:

The Center for Safety in the Arts, 5 Beekman Street, Suite 1030, New York, NY 10038; 212-227-6220, is a national clearinghouse for research and education on hazards in the visual arts, performing arts, education facilities, and museums. Contact them if you have questions about any of the products you are using.

• *Keep your work area separate from your living area.* Your kitchen is not the best place to work. Set up a hot plate in your basement or garage and do not use pots, spoons, cups, or a microwave oven that will later be used to whip up Sunday supper.

• *Read your MSDSs.* By law, all dye manufacturers must provide you with a print-out called a Material Safety Data Sheet, which details the known and potential safety hazards of each dye. Because different chemicals are used to create different colors, each dye you use will have its own MSDS data. Read them all.

• *Avoid toxic materials if/when possible.* For example, try to use water-based rather than oil-based solvents.

• *Don't work in areas that have drapes and rugs.* They can collect airbornes.

• *Keep powdered materials and liquid dyes in sealed jars.* Be sure shelving is secure. Bulk items should be on the floor instead of up on shelves.

• *Adequate ventilation is critical.* Do not work with a fan or open window behind you. If you use a fan, make sure it is in front of you and your work, and set it on *exhaust*. Wear a face mask, even if you work outside.

• *Keep a fire extinguisher and emergency first-aid kit and emergency phone numbers nearby.*

Tools of the Trade

When you dye fabric, you will need a variety of tools. Before you purchase any supplies, look around your house to see if you can recycle objects you already own.

Newburyport artist Lucinda Cathcart discovered that her grandmother's old lace-curtain stretchers were the ideal shape and size for preparing silk for hand-painting. Arashi *shibori* artist Judith Content takes advantage of her Sonoma Valley, California, address and uses glass wine bottles instead of poles around which to wrap her silk. Carter Smith outfitted his basement studio—from his 10-burner cast-iron stove to his stainless-steel discharge vats and prep table—by combing newspaper advertisements for restaurant supply auctions.

Whether you use new or recycled items, remember that once you appropriate something for a dyeing project, you should never use the object for any culinary purpose.

Another important caveat: Stick with non-porous, non-corrosive materials such as glass, stainless steel, or enamel when at all possible. Avoid plastic containers if you plan to re-use the containers later for different colored dyes. Plastic is absorbent and will allow residual dye to leach out and adulterate other dyes you put in the container later.

Fabric Preparation

If you put a length of fabric under a microscope, the lens would reveal spots, uneven amounts of sizing, and bits of fuzz left over from the weaving process, any of which could cause your dye job to come out splotchy and uneven.

Although many suppliers sell pre-laundered or "artist-ready" fabric, *always* pre-wash your fabric first with *Synthrapol®*, a liquid detergent favored for textile dyeing, or other recommended soap (such as *Shaklee Scouring Soap* or *Amway* soap). Do not use any soaps that contain sulfites, bleach, softeners, or optical brighteners, or other additives. They will ruin your work. Scoured fabric can be dried and set aside for future use, or kept damp (depending on technique to be used). For assembly-line work with damp fabric, fold individual lengths of fabric into smaller sections and store in plastic zip-lock bags until ready to use. Don't store too long or the fabric will get musty or mildewy.

MATERIALS CHECKLIST

A precisely calibrated scale
for measuring powdered dyes. This is a must.

Smallish containers
in which to mix and store your dye solution: Glass jars left over from baby food, jelly, or condiments; plastic or paper cups.

Measuring, mixing, and stirring tools:
Popsicle sticks and bamboo skewers; stainless steel spoons; chemists' glass pipettes.

Containers to dispense your dye solution:
Plastic squeeze bottles with protective tips (to prevent evaporation) are ideal.

Containers for dipping/immersing.

Drying rack or clothesline, wooden or plastic clothes pins.

Stainless steel vegetable steamer, tongs, long-handled spoon.

Plastic wrap.

Rubber and cotton gloves.
(Cotton worn under the rubber will help cut down on perspiration.)

Blank newsprint paper or kraft paper.

Old towels.

Stretchers, embroidery hoops, padded surface, mesh screen.

Dressmaker pins.

Cotton or nylon cord, rubber bands,
stuff from hospital supply stores.

A protected, preferably non-porous surface
on which to apply the dye. Firm surfaces are best: Plexiglas, stainless steel, an old sheet of linoleum. Layers of newspaper or paper towel on top of a plastic shower curtain are also good.

Kitchen timer with a loud bell.

Thermometer
to monitor the temperature of the dye bath.

Assorted paint brushes: bristled, chiseled, foam-tipped, etc.

Calculator, index cards, and paper and pencil
to work out measurements for your dye solutions.

Metric conversion charts
(see Appendix).

There are usually two steps involved in preparing a dye for use: one that should be done in advance, and one done at the time you are ready to dye. Although instructions will vary from brand to brand, the general procedure is outlined here. (Please note that the following information assumes you are using acid or reactive dyes and not one-shot types of dyes that require no mixing or additives.)

Make a dye stock solution by measuring the required amount of dye, and store the solution in tightly sealed containers.

Prepare your dye color as desired (here, a violet is being obtained by mixing blue and fuschia).

Step One:

Mixing a dye solution. Most professional-quality dyes are sold in powdered form, although a few fiber-reactive types, some acid dyes, and several direct dyes are also available in liquid concentrate form. Liquid dyes cost more, but the time involved in mixing is something many artists do not want to deal with.

Although powdered dyes do not have to be pre-pared in advance, it is far safer and more efficient time-wise to mix them into a liquid concentrate several days before dyeing. To do this, measure the required amount of dye (the amount will vary depending upon the type and color of dye used) into a cup and slowly stir in a tablespoon of warm water. Stir to a paste-like consistency, making sure all lumps are removed. Slowly add one-half cup hot water and stir until all particles are dissolved. (Do not use hot water for MX-type reactive dyes—the dyes will react with water before they get to the fabric.) Slowly add another half-cup of water. Store the solution in tightly sealed bottles.

The shelf life of dye solution will vary depending on the type of dye used and how it is stored. In general, the stock should be used within six months. Shelf life is improved if the stock is stored in a cool, dark area and is well sealed.

Once a dye solution has bypassed its shelf life, it may still have the ability to impart some color to the fiber, but you won't get the same color you got months before. Other dyes actually deteriorate, turn slimy, or crystallize into a non-soluble salt once they have been in contact with water for a period of time. Run a test swatch through a sample bath of any dye you have questions about. If you are dyeing a small item, you may be able to still make use of an old solution.

Some separation will occur and a sediment may accumulate in the bottom of the jar if any solution sits for a while—even a few days. If this happens, gently and briefly warm the solution in a double-boiler and stir. Keep in mind that with too much exposure to heat, some of the water will evaporate and alter the color of the dye somewhat.

Step Two:

Mixing concentrated dye into a dye bath or a chemical-water mix. Whether you use liquid dyes or mix up your own stock solutions from powdered dye, the liquid dye must ultimately be mixed with water and a number of other inexpensive additives in order for the dye to be effective. The additives for acid- and fiber-reactive dyes vary according to the class of dye you are using and the type of dyeing you plan to do.

Some suppliers sell pre-measured additives in individual packets; others sell bulk quantities of the individual items. At the time you make an order or purchase, be sure to ask your salesperson about the following:

Acid Dye Additives:

Salt (plain, non-iodized table salt; other types of salt contain trace minerals that can affect exhaustion).

Acidic medium such as distilled white vinegar (check the label to make sure the strength is five percent; some generic vinegars have only a three percent strength); citric acid (sold in crystals); or ammonium sulfate (available from suppliers). The latter two are preferred by many textile artists because they lack the acrid smell characteristic of vinegar.

Synthrapol® (a mild, neutral surfactant). In

❣ *Tip:*

When mixing powders, it is important to wear a respirator mask to avoid ingesting airborne particles.

Sample Measurements for Stock Solutions (Per cup of water)

Type of Dye	Full Depth of Shade	Medium Tint	Light Tint	Pale Tint
Acid	2 tsp*	1 tsp	1/2 tsp	1/4 tsp
Fiber-reactive	4 tsp*	2 tsp	1 tsp	1/2 tsp

*Note: For the deepest black, double the amounts indicated here.

Scour Power

addition to being used for gentle cleaning of the material (see fabric preparation, page 15), the use of *Synthrapol®* in the dye bath enhances the "wetting out" of a fiber. This ensures maximum absorption of the dye.

These three ingredients can be mixed together in advance, according to suppliers' instructions, and can be kept on hand for three months.

Fiber-Reactive Dye Additives:

Synthrapol® (see above).

Alkali activator/fixative such as soda ash (also known as sodium carbonate, commercial washing soda, or sal soda); tri-sodium phosphate (TSP); or any brand-name activator sold by your supplier. Do not use the washing soda sold in the laundry detergent section of your supermarket. It contains brightening agents that will counteract the effectiveness of the dye.

Salt or Urea (ammonium carbamate), depending on the application technique. Salt is used for immersion, also known as long-liquor ratio dyeing. Urea is used for direct application techniques such as painting (also known as short-liquor ratio dyeing). This will be discussed in greater detail in the Painterly Techniques chapter.

Water softener such as *Calgon* or *Metaphos* (if your water is hard).

❧ *Tip:*

How hard is your water? Hardness is caused by metallic ions that prevent deep, level dyeing. To counteract this problem, you may want to add a softener such as Calgon *or* Metaphos *to the water.*

The following recipe for an all-purpose pre-wash comes from PRO-Chemical and Dye Company in Fall River, Massachusetts, a major supplier of dyes for textile artists:

For each pound (454 grams) of fabric, add 1/2 teaspoon (2.5 ml) each of *Synthrapol®* (to loosen debris) and soda ash, activator, or commercial washing soda (see above) to 140°F (60°C) water (maximum liquor ratio of 20:1 or 30:1).

Agitate in the machine for 15 minutes, then rinse in warm water.

Dye immediately while still damp, or let fabric dry and set aside. When ready to dye, briefly submerge cloth in water to re-dampen.

There are three main variables to consider when mixing your dyes:

1. **The amount and type of fabric used.**
2. **The method of dyeing being used.**
3. **The color and intensity of color you desire.**

Amount of Fabric

Most instructions for professional-quality dyes are based on the total weight of the fabric you plan to dye, rather than the linear measurement. Instructions will interchangeably use the term "weight of goods," or the abbreviation "W.O.G."

Along with weight of goods, it is important to consider the fabric's density when deciding on the amount of concentrate to use. One pound of a densely-woven, coarse fabric such as Thai silk will take up dye more slowly than a similar amount of cotton jersey (t-shirt material). To see for yourself, mix up a small dye bath and dip different types of fabric in for the same length of time. Let them dry and compare the color. This will give you an idea of how much additional concentrate you will need to achieve the desired results.

Dyeing Method

The two basic types of dyeing are immersion and direct application.

For immersion dyeing, as with cooking pasta, the fabric should have plenty of room to move around in the pot and have an ample amount of liquid to bathe in. (EXCEPTION: If you want a mottled effect, tighter quarters are a plus). Consequently, you will sometimes see this method referred to as "long-liquor ratio" dyeing.

If you are going to apply your dye directly by painting, dribbling, spraying, or sponging, you need less water. Hence, the term "short-liquor ratio" is often used to describe direct application methods.

Instructions from the dye supplier always include the recommended liquor ratio, often abbreviated L:R. This refers to the amount of water recommended for each dry pound of fabric you plan to dye. Generally, the liquor ratio for immersion-dyeing yarn and very, very sheer fabrics such as georgette is anywhere from 30 to 1 (expressed as 30:1) to 40 to 1. For denser fabrics a ratio of 20:1 is advised.

If using a direct-application method, you need a more concentrated solution of dye than you would use for immersion. Again, consult the instructions that come from your supplier for the proper recipe.

Color & Intensity

As you experiment with dyes, you will discover that all colors are not created equal. It takes half as much red dye, for example, to achieve the same depth of shade as it takes to get a similar value of yellow or blue. To achieve the blackest black, you will generally need to use three times more dye than you need for other colors.

A Pound is a Pound is a Pound

If you don't have a scale handy, the following list gives the one-pound (454 grams) equivalents of several different items:

Three adult-size t-shirts

One adult-size sweatshirt

Three to six yards/meters of fabric (e.g., cotton broadcloth runs about four yards/meters to the pound)

Twelve 36-inch squares (one square meter each) of silk chiffon

The showcase sections on the following pages illustrate that few artists limit themselves to the use of just one textile-dyeing technique. Immersion, discharge, block printing, and over-dyeing are often employed in the same piece to give a work depth and complexity.

Rather than serving as an end in themselves, therefore, we hope that the techniques shown will provide food for thought and serve as a launching pad for your own creative ventures in textile dyeing.

Along with using multiple techniques—say, discharge with *batik*—the following are just some of the ways you can add extra interest to your fabric before or after executing the primary surface design technique.

Surface Flair

With all of the techniques that follow, remember that dye is transparent. Whenever it is placed on top of another color—either by direct application or immersion—a new color will result. Because of this, many surface techniques are best applied to white or light-colored backgrounds.

Salt, sugar, alcohol. While the dye is still wet on your fabric, you can create interesting effects by sprinkling salt or granulated sugar over the cloth. The dye will be attracted to the granules and will make an interesting, diffused pattern as it moves toward them. The effects with salt will be much more pronounced than with sugar.

Sugar water (a simple syrup made by heating four cups of water with one cup of sugar until it dissolves) can be painted over fabric before it is dyed to create a different diffused effect. After applying the solution to stretched fabric (you can brush it, roll it, or spatter it on), add the dye (you can spray, sponge, or spatter it, too, or use a brush to create specific shapes). Allow the fabric to dry completely before rinsing and fixing.

Alcohol can be painted or sponged over dry, dyed fabric to create a dreamy, three-dimensional effect. Wherever the alcohol is dabbed or brushed, the color will thin and lighten as the dye moves away from the point of contact. A halo or corona of darker color will outline and define the area where the alcohol did not reach. (Note: Be cautious when using alcohol, as it is combustible and can be a fire hazard. Also avoid breathing the fumes—they can be toxic.)

Sponging, ragging, combing, rolling. Using natural sponges, crumpled-up rags, or small paint rollers, apply thickened dyes (see Chapter 3) to your fabric. Marbled effects can be created by rolling or sponging at least three colors onto one fabric.

❦ *Tip:*

What exactly is "room temperature"? If you tend to walk around bare-footed in the winter, your notion of room temperature will be very different from that of someone who shivers when it's 60°F. In the world of dyeing, temperature is not subjective. Room temperature means approximately 75° to 95°F. If you are working in a space colder than this, be prepared for some disappointing results.

Spraying, spattering, etc. A little concentrated dye stock in a spray bottle, airbrush, or the head of a toothbrush can be blown, flecked, sprayed, or spattered onto fabric for an interesting effect. When you use this approach, play it safe: wear goggles and a mask to prevent splats and flecks from making it onto and into your body.

Pigments, paints for texture. Pigments sit on the surface of your fabric and can be used to give extra texture and dimension to your work. Dip a bunched-up paper towel, a crumpled-up rag, or a sponge in a small amount of pigment and dab it over the dry, dyed fabric for a final surface touch. Or use wood blocks, stencils, or other templates. Paint a thin wash of pigment over the entire fabric and then comb, brush, or thumb-print over the entire surface.

Over-Dyeing

This is a method popular with quilters who want to unify several commercially printed fabrics—small calicoes or geometrics, for example—by submerging them in a commonly colored dyebath. Overdyeing can produce interesting shades and effects.

Because dyes are transparent, the images on the original fabric will always remain visible, albeit slightly colored by the new layer of dye—and the background will take on a new color depending on the original color of the fabric and that of the dye used.

In general, it is best to use a lightly tinted dyebath, especially if the background color of the fabric is something other than white.

Remember to scour the fabric completely before dyeing. Commercially printed cottons tend to be heavily infused with sizing to give them body on the bolt. This sizing will prevent proper absorption of the dye.

Stitching

Many artists have found that cutting apart dyed fabric and reassembling it collage-style makes for an interesting effect. Embroidery, quilting, appliqué, and other fine stitchery techniques can also reiterate the color and textural statement made by the dyeing process. Consider using metallic threads with metallic pigments, or try pulling out some of the weft (horizontal) threads in the fabric to create a lacy effect.

❦ *Tip:*

Consider the temperature of more than your room. Your dyes, work surface, even your fabric need to be the same temperature to ensure optimum results. If you store damp fabric in a cool basement, for example, make sure you bring it into the studio so that it reaches proper temperature before you start to work.

Immersion Tips

❧ *Tip:*

When using the steam method to set dyes, condensation that accumulates on the lid of your pot could drip down onto the fabric and cause streaking. To prevent this, lay several terry cloth washcloths or several layers of newspaper on top of the dyed cloth.

• It is always best to put damp, rather than dry, fabric into the dye bath. This ensures even dyeing.

• When dyeing several different pieces in succession, remember that there will be less water with each subsequent dip. If you don't replenish the water, each piece you dye will come out darker than the first. Moreover, if using acid dyes, the concentration of vinegar and salt in the dye bath will get stronger as the volume of water decreases. This can lead to yellowing and possibly even burning of the fiber. For the sake of uniformity, it is better to use a larger dye bath that can accommodate all the pieces you want to dye at one time.

• To avoid streaking and splashing, fold the fabric into soft accordion pleats before lowering it into the bath.

• Stir the fabric in a figure-eight motion to ensure an even flow of dye around the material.

Direct Application Tips

• Reactive dyes are often mixed with a water solution containing urea to help keep the dye from drying out too quickly, thus ensuring a longer reaction time. Once mixed with urea, fiber-reactive dyes should be used within five days.

• Once applied to the fabric, the wet dye always looks darker than it will be when dry. Don't skimp on the dye at this stage.

• The tools you use for direct application are limitless: high-quality bristle brushes, inexpensive chiseled foam-tipped applicators, bulb basters or syringes, air brushes or spray bottles. (If using the latter, be sure to wear a mask to avoid ingesting airborne dye mist.) Be inventive.

• Because you will be working with several colors at the same time, make sure you have plenty of wipe-up cloths on hand. Also be sure to keep your hands clean. Check them and your work surface for stray dribbles that could work their way onto the cloth.

• Always be aware of the surface beneath the fabric you are dyeing. Either make sure the cloth is suspended high enough above the surface to prevent it from absorbing drips of color that have leaked through, or place the fabric directly on top of a well-padded, absorbent surface.

• When painting with *gutta* on silk scarves with handrolled edges, remember that there is extra thickness at the edges. Make sure you apply enough dye and/or *gutta* to soak through all the layers. Another neat trick is to draw a border with *gutta* completely around the perimeter of the scarf a few inches away from the edge; then you can dye the edge a solid color without having to worry about the *gutta* edge.

What about the Washing Machine?

If you are interested in trying this method, the key variable to check is the temperature of your hot water. The machine should be able to produce a minimum temperature of 140°F. If it can't, you may not get the results you desire (especially with acid dyes). Fiber-reactive dyes tend to produce better overall results.

Generally, you will need to use slightly more dye to achieve the same results in a washing machine as you would with stove-top methods. Also do not be tempted to pack the machine full. Although most home washing machines can accommodate up to eight pounds of fabric at one time, it is best to limit each load to five pounds to ensure plenty of room for the fabric to move around.

Also, do not look upon machine dyeing as a way to push a button, walk away and do something else for the next thirty minutes. The best results are obtained by intervening several times during the wash cycle to redistribute the load, pour in the needed additives, and stopping the machine several times to allow the fabric to steep.

Fixing, Finishing, and Clean-Up

The moment of truth has arrived: the timer bell has rung, your *magnum opus* is ready to be rinsed and dried. You toss it into the washing machine, turn on the rinse cycle, and sit back and relax. Right? Wrong. There is still a chance for your dye job to come out botched. Rinsing techniques vary according to the dye used and should be followed carefully to make sure the dye doesn't end up fading or bleeding after the first wash.

In general, fabric or fibers colored with acid dyes can be rinsed in several changes of warm water in a sink or pail until the water runs clear. They can then be laundered and machine-dried to soften and intensify the colors.

When you are finished dyeing, be kind to the environment and dispose of your dye baths properly. Both acid and fiber-reactive dyes can be poured down a sink, but should be neutralized beforehand. Acid dyes are neutralized by the addition of baking soda (approximately 3 teaspoons of soda for each liter of water); fiber-reactive dyes are neutralized with vinegar. The amount of vinegar to use depends on the strength of your dye solution. For black dye baths mix in approximately 1/4 cup vinegar for each quart/liter of bath. Two to three teaspoons of vinegar are adequate for the lightest dye baths.

❧ *Tip:*

Fiber-reactive dyes should be rinsed out in 75-95°F water to start, followed by warm water, followed by hot.

CHAPTER 3

Painterly Techniques

MARIANNA HAMILTON ROSS
Red Stemmed Philodendron, *32" x 40" silk*

Textile artists have been painting dyes directly on fabric for thousands of years. But in the last decade or so, due in great part to the widespread availability of highly reactive dyes that can be applied and cured at room temperature, painterly techniques have eclipsed immersion dyeing as the favored artistic method of coloring and patterning material.

Along with ease of application, painterly methods are decidedly friendlier to the environment. Applied directly, the dyes use less water and generally less energy than immersion methods. And because you can see your work as you go along, there are fewer unhappy surprises at the end of the dyeing cycle.

Painterly techniques share several common steps. The fabric is first laid flat and stretched tight or pinned to a work surface; next, several different colors of dyes are painted on and allowed to dry or cure before being rinsed.

Variations in painting techniques will result in decidedly different results. You can use one of the following methods alone, or combine several to create intricate, multi-dimensional works.

Painting With Liquid Resists

There are many types of liquid resists available today—the oldest and most familiar of which is *gutta*. Liquid resists penetrate the fiber wherever they are applied and prevent the dye from moving beyond them. By outlining your design first with a liquid resist, you can then paint inside the defined area and the dye will stop when it reaches the resist barrier.

After the painting is finished, the resist is removed with either a solvent (*gutta*) or warm water depending on resist used.

Liquid resist can be applied with a brush, but it is most commonly dispensed from a small plastic squeeze-bottle. The nozzle of the bottle can be outfitted with different-sized tips, which control the thickness of the flow.

DAVID AND LINDA FRANCE HARTGE/KALEIDOSILK
Ginkgo/Fan,
detail of square scarf

David Hartge

The Great *Gutta* Debate

Which is better: solvent- or water-based resists? No two artists agree. Some feel that traditional solvent-based *gutta* takes a bit more skill to master. It can get thick if it sits around too long and needs to be thinned to the proper consistency with mineral spirits. Mix it too thin and it won't block the flow of dye; if it is too thick, it won't penetrate the silk. Because of the fumes produced, solvent-based *guttas* need to be applied in a well-ventilated area.

Water-soluble resists do not require any special materials to remove them from the fabric. However, some artists, such as David and Linda France Hartge, feel that they do not block the dye and hold a fine line as effectively as *gutta*. "This is not the case as much when you are working on very thin silk," David Hartge notes, "but for slightly heavier fabrics we feel the penetration of solvent-based *gutta* is much better."

Thickened Dyes

If thickened to the viscosity of honey, dye remains primarily where it is placed on the fabric and does not migrate. This gives the artist more time to shape the image and produce interesting layered effects.

Although many substances can be used to thicken dye, the most popular one used today is sodium alginate, otherwise known as seaweed extract. Sold in powdered form, sodium alginate is mixed with water and allowed to sit until it plumps up the water to a gelatinous consistency. It is then mixed with the liquid dye and chemical water (see Chapter 8). The additives required will depend upon whether you are using an acid or fiber-reactive dye, so check with your supplier to make sure you use the correct ingredients.

In addition to painting images, you can use thickened dyes to add surface finishes to cloth the same way you do to furniture. Sponging, ragging, combing, and thumb-printing are just some of the possible methods that can be used instead of, or in addition to, painting.

Watercolor Technique

With the watercolor technique, liquid dye solution, made without thickeners, is painted onto wet or dry fabric with quick, controlled strokes. The dye wicks into the surrounding fibers and takes on a soft, diffused look as it stops migrating outward from the original point of application. Additional layers of color are applied after previous ones are completely dry, or may be applied while the first layer is still wet. Fine detail is achieved with smaller and dryer brushes.

PEGGY RUSSELL/
IRO DESIGN
Silk crepe painted with thickened dye

LUCINDA CATHCART
Rainbow painted silk, stamped with gold pigment

Art of Light

27

Gutta Resist

David Hartge

DAVID AND LINDA FRANCE HARTGE/KALEIDOSILK
36" x 36" **Hibiscus** *scarf, detail*

Unlike the free-flowing styles of Peggy Russell and Lucinda Cathcart, David and Linda France Hartge's work is highly representational and reflects masterful precision and fine detail. Their signature look is achieved with the use of *gutta* resist, and wet-on-wet application of acid dyes combined with water and alcohol.

David and Linda work together to contribute to the conceptualization of each design they create. A fascination with the shapes and colors of nature strongly influences all of the their work. Hibiscus and orchids are frequently in bloom throughout their suburban Washington, D.C., home and serve as models for the blossoms they add to the silk. "Another of our favorite themes is mixed vegetables," David Hartge adds. "We'll have peas floating in space or hopping out of their pods." Along with adding a whimsical flavor to otherwise intensely precise imagery, he notes, "It's a license to deal with drips."

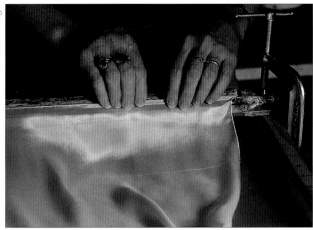

David Hartge

Materials & Equipment:

Silk
*(avoid textured or patterned silks such
as jacquards or noile types)*

Liquid acid dye

Alcohol

Water

Calligraphic brushes
(in a variety of sizes)

Silk stretcher

C-clamps

Clear and black solvent-based *gutta*

Plastic applicator bottles
and a variety of tips/nibs

1 After pre-washing your silk (lighter, less textured silk such as crepe de chine, rather than jacquard or embossed silk is better when using *gutta*), stretch and suspend it above the work surface. The fabric cannot sit directly on the table or else the dye will wick directly over the *gutta* lines. David and Linda use stretchers that are a combination of pins secured with C-clamps.

🐝 *Tip:*

*David and Linda use twelve basic colors of H. DuPont (from Paris) liquid acid dye; from these they can mix more than 100 colors. For each color used, they add alcohol and water in equal parts to the liquid dye. As you will see in **Step 7**, it is very important to know in advance what colors you are going to use and to have those jars open and ready and the brushes nearby.*

2 An essential tool for achieving crisp, defined lines is the use of a straightedge that acts as an arm rest for drawing, as well as a ruler to make straight lines. David and Linda use a smooth piece of lumber that is cut longer and wider than the stretching frame. Reposition it along the silk as you move, making sure the *gutta* is completely dry before you move it. (Solvent-based *gutta* dries very quickly on silk.)

3 Assemble the materials and prepare the *gutta*. Because *gutta* tends to thicken overnight, thoroughly flush out the squeeze bottle before each use and redilute as necessary with mineral spirits. The *gutta* should be able to flow, enabling you to move your hand in a graceful arc as you draw. Ideally, there should be no skips or bubbles, and the *gutta* should be absorbed by the silk and should not spread noticeably. If the line seems to broaden out, the *gutta* is too thin. If it is too thick, it won't flow and won't seem to penetrate.

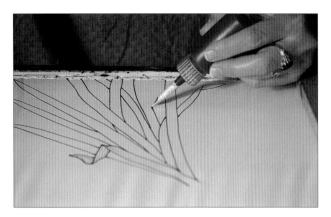

4 It is important to plan your design, placing design elements in key fields such as corners and the center so as to balance the page in terms of composition. Begin your outlining by placing these key elements on the silk first. Here, Linda places foliage motifs in the corners of their project.

6 If you want any area to be white, leave that space alone and add depth and texture by using touches of pale, pale pinks, blues, or grays to create the effect of shadows. While working, if you want to preserve a space and ensure that the contouring dyes won't bleed toward it, you can take a brush with pure alcohol on it and dab it into the area you want to remain white. Then, if a colored dye comes near it while it is wet, the alcohol will repel it. Keep wetting the area with dabs of alcohol while you work, because the repelling action will stop once it has dried.

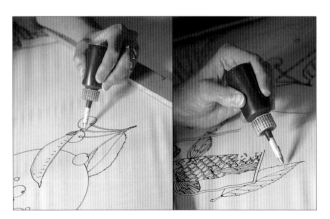

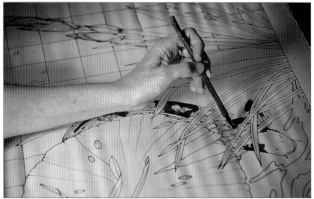

5 Outline the design with clear or black *gutta*, changing nibs as needed to define thicker or thinner outline areas according to the design. (Some artists prefer to use quilter's pens to map out their design prior to this step.) Clear *gutta* is best used for images that will be painted with light colors: pink or white, etc., for apple blossoms. Although clear *gutta* is not invisible after being applied, it can be difficult to see in natural daylight, so be sure to work where the artificial light supply is plentiful.

7 Fill in the colored areas using calligraphic-style brushes with bamboo handles. Ideally you want a brush that will come to a very, very fine point and hold a lot of dye. Begin by painting all the items that have the same basic color. If, for example, your design includes cherries, a fish, and a tomato, color all of them first, layering color upon color as desired to achieve depth and texture.

8 Next, apply background color, beginning with the areas that are adjacent to other colored images. Use a small amount of dye on your brush initially because it will be drawn toward the colored images, and a too-wet brush could cause the dye to skip the *gutta* line if the line is not strong enough. If layering colors, you must work quickly and finish an area before the dye dries out. Otherwise, if you add a color to one that is already dry, you get what is called a tide line. The dye gets pushed up to a spot and stops, creating a jagged line.

9 If you are concerned about the integrity of the *gutta* line (a consideration in areas where you used the finest nib) paint the lighter areas first. That way if the *gutta* doesn't hold you can wait for the dye to dry and then redraw the *gutta* line again to make it heavier. With the checkerboard, for example, David and Linda put down the blue first and then waited to see how well it held the line. If some blue spilled over onto the black, that would have been easier to correct than if black had spilled onto an area that was supposed to be light blue.

10 Once the painting is finished, allow it to dry completely. No rinsing will be needed. Place a length of newsprint or kraft paper over the fabric, roll it over a firm cylinder (David suggests chicken wire), and steam for three and a half hours. "We used to steam for less time, since the manufacturer says anywhere from 30 minutes on is acceptable, but red and black are very hard to fasten into the silk. We found that longer is definitely better."

If you don't want to steam the silk immediately—David and Linda wait until they have ten or so yards to put in the steamer—be sure the silk does not get exposed to anything wet. At this point, the dye is still indeterminate and will spot if even a drop of water falls on it.

 Tip:

Dry cleaning will lighten black gutta to a battleship-gray color. If you are making items that will be sold to customers, and part of what they fall in love with is that distinctive black gutta line, make sure you either label the garment "hand-wash only," or else dry clean it ahead of sale.

Metallic guttas have a tendency to turn rubbery and peel away after dry cleaning. David and Linda never use them for that reason.

Thickened Dyes

Art of Light

PEGGY RUSSELL/IRO DESIGN
Hand-painted silk

Boston resident Peggy Russell, a 32-year-old graduate of the School of the Museum of Fine Arts at Tufts University, has carved a comfortable niche in the art-to-wear genre. While a student, she specialized in textile printing, painting, and Egyptian art, and the colorful, off-kilter designs she paints onto silk and cotton canvas reflect an innovative fusion of several design disciplines.

Favoring fiber-reactive dyes for their brilliance and depth of color, Russell paints directly onto the fabric, layering colors in a wet-on-wet process that enables the shades to blend and diffuse. Rather than using a resist such as *gutta* or wax to constrain the flow of dye, she blends her dyes with a seaweed extract alginate that plumps up to a gelatinous consistency when mixed with water and other natural ingredients. The thickened dye is then placed into squeeze bottles and plastic jars that are kept at table-side as she works.

Russell's imagery is playful, even funky, but rooted in a strong sense of fine art history. Inspired by artists such as De Chirico and Matisse, she puts her own spin on motifs that range from junk food to botanicals to hieroglyphs and totems. The painted fabrics are ultimately sewn into swing tops, scarves, men's ties, vests, and backpacks. Her company, IRO Design, is now in its eighth year and counts among its clients Nordstrom's, Barney's, The Signature Galleries, and numerous specialty shops throughout the U.S. and Canada.

Art of Light

1 After adding water to powdered *Procion MX* fiber-reactive dye according to the manufacturer's directions, Russell adds a seaweed thickener, or alginate, to bring the dyes to a consistency that will prevent them from bleeding into the fabric. For use on chiffon, the dye mixture should be the viscosity of honey. For heavier-weight fabrics, Russell suggests using more thickener to bring the dye to the consistency of mayonnaise. It is important to experiment ahead of time with scrap fabric to determine how much bleeding and saturation will occur with varying consistencies of thickened dye.

Materials & Equipment:

Dye concentrate or powdered dye
mixed to solution according to manufacturer's directions

Sodium alginate*

Chemical water
(urea, soda ash/activator, etc.)

Plastic squeeze bottles

Paint brushes

White canvas or heavy twill
for drop cloth

Quilter's pins

Silk chiffon or crepe de chine

Steamer

Newsprint or kraft paper

Cardboard tube

__Note:__ If you are using reactive dyes, only alginates should be used for thickening. Other thickeners are cellulose derivatives and will react with the dye and subsequently wash off.

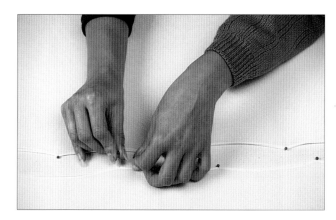

2 Russell stretches the silk chiffon taut and pins it to a solid, heavy surface that has been covered with pre-washed dry white canvas. Ball-headed quilting pins or T-pins are recommended to anchor the silk.

3-4 An outline of the design is applied to the fabric using a plastic squeeze bottle. Use a moderate amount of pressure; the dye should soak into the fabric and not sit on the surface. With a paint brush, catch any "beads" of dye sitting on the surface and draw them out to incorporate the excess dye into the fabric.

To create a drop-shadow effect, Russell adds an outline of charcoal-gray dye around certain areas of the images.

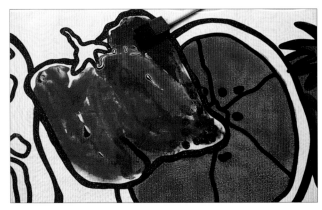

5 When the outline dye has dried (this will vary depending on the fabric used; for silk chiffon, the dye should be dry in one to two hours), Russell applies the first color with a chisel-tipped foam brush. The color may be brushed directly over the black outline. Vary the pressure on the brush to achieve a range of color saturation. Because much of the dye will bleed through the chiffon and onto the drop-cloth canvas below, it is very important to saturate the cloth completely. After painting one layer of dye onto the fabric, wait a few minutes and then reapply as necessary to push the dye into the fibers.

6 While the first color is still wet, Russell adds a "wash" of a second or even a third color directly on top of it to achieve subtle tonal variations and prevent the image from looking flat. The colors chosen are not formulaic but rather up to the artist's discretion, and the resulting blends are very much like those achieved in watercolor painting. It is important to move quickly and to add the layer colors while the undercoats are still wet. Otherwise, the resulting look will be harsh and choppy rather than diffused.

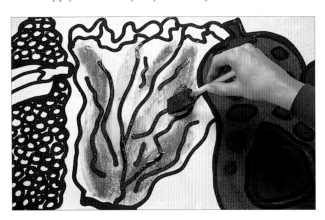

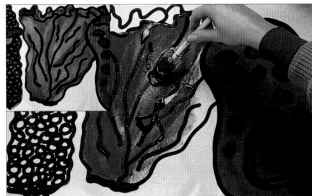

7 Russell paints a wash of plain alginate over some images prior to brushing on the dye, applying globs in some areas and thick streaks in others. The alginate acts somewhat like a resist by preventing varying levels of dye absorption depending on how thickly it is applied.

8 As the dye and alginate dries, the color of the image painted with alginate will take on a translucent, lighter effect than the surrounding areas not exposed to alginate.

9 Improvisation is part of the artist's prerogative. Here, Russell decides the grapes need a wash of color that has not already been prepared. Using a plastic lid as a palette, she spoons three different dyes onto the surface and lightly swirls them together, then stipples them onto the grapes. Using a light hand and feathering motion, she blends and smooths this wash to ensure that the individual colors retain their own integrity and delicately diffuse into each other.

10 Russell applies the background color last, although it can also be applied immediately after outlining. As the dye dries, the colors intensify and actually seem to separate from each other. This characteristic of fiber-reactive dyes, says Russell, is the reason she prefers using them for her projects.

11 When dry (three to four hours for chiffon, longer for heavier fabrics), the top layer is peeled away from the canvas, leaving a mirror image of itself on the drop cloth below. The chiffon is then spread smoothly onto an underlayer of cotton sheeting, carefully rolled over a cardboard tube, and placed in a steamer for three hours to set the dye.

12 While the silk is in the steamer, the drop-cloth canvas is embellished with additional lines, doctored up to fill in bare areas, and then treated to a steam bath, too. When dry, it will be stitched into vests, roll-brim hats, back packs, and tote bags, which are in as much demand as the painted silk.

Watercolor Technique

Art of light

LUCINDA CATHCART
Silk crepe de chine painted with
Procion® fiber-reactive dye

During her first year as a student at Rochester Institute of Technology's American Artistry program, Lucinda Cathcart had a Damascus experience. "I sat down at a loom," she says, "and I was hooked. I immediately called my parents up and told them that I was switching my major from graphic design to textiles. They thought I was crazy."

She *was* crazy—crazy about fiber arts of all sorts. After receiving a degree in textile design, Cathcart and her husband relocated to the historic coastal town of Newburyport, Massachusetts. Here, surrounded by 200-year-old mercantile buildings and gas-lit sidewalks, Cathcart began to experiment with painting on silk. "I played around with *gutta*, did some silk screening, and finally realized that I liked this method of working the best."

The method she refers to is a watercolor technique, in which she applies a thin solution of dye onto tightly stretched silk, adding subsequent layers after the previous ones are dry. "I know that many artists like to control where the dye goes," she says, "but I love to see what happens when the color bleeds and travels into the fibers along whatever path it chooses." The path is not totally random, she notes; with practice one can predict with some accuracy how far the dye will spread and how diffuse it will look.

Art of light

1-2 After tightly stretching her fabric onto a wooden frame (at one time they were her grandmother's lace curtain stretchers), Cathcart uses a square, flat tipped Japanese brush and blocks out preliminary shapes onto the silk. The dye will wick quickly into the fabric—"like water on tissue," Cathcart says—so do not overload your brush. After dipping the brush in the paint, blot it on several thicknesses of paper towels to remove excess that might drip off and create unwanted splatters. Use a firm hand as you paint to minimize paint flicking or spattering onto the surrounding fabric.

Materials & Equipment:

Silk
(of your choice)
Liquid fiber-reactive dye
Stretchers
Brushes
(Flat-headed or foam-tipped variety, plus a variety of pointed-tip brushes.)
Cardboard roll
Kraft paper or newsprint

Tip:

Watercolor paintings derive their luminous quality from repeated layerings of color, Cathcart explains. It is the same with painting on silk. She never knows ahead of time what colors she is going to want to use, and prefers to mix as she works. For the sake of speed and convenience, she uses liquid Procion® H dye rather than a powdered form. Cathcart maintains an inventory of seven different dye bases—red, fuchsia, navy, cobalt, two yellows, brown, black, and turquoise—and mixes small amounts together with water combined with urea and softener (per instructions provided by the manufacturer) in glass baby-food jars as she works.

3 The dye must be completely dry before adding subsequent colors. Depending on the fabric being used, drying time can be anywhere from ten minutes to 24 hours.

4 Choosing deeper shades that complement the shapes already painted, Cathcart uses the same square-headed brush to add foliage to some areas and shadow lines in broad strokes. When adding color on top of color, remember that dyes are transparent; even when dry, a blue layered on top of a yellow will "read" as a greenish shade.

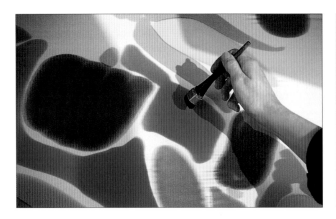

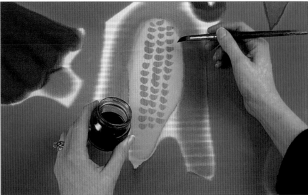

5 The background color is now applied to the thoroughly dry fabric. Cathcart begins defining the area to be filled in by placing her brush no more than 3/4 of an inch away from any of the shapes she has already painted. This will allow the dye to wick inwards toward the painted shapes without bleeding onto them. Then she fills in the defined area with more outline color.

6 After the final layer of basic color has dried, Cathcart switches from a "wet brush" to a "dry brush" technique—a method familiar to watercolorists who paint on paper. Using a pointed-tipped brush, dip the tip lightly into the dye so that the color is drawn up no more than a few millimeters into the bristles. This allows for greater control and minimizes bleeding into the surrounding fabric.

Work quickly, keeping in mind that because dye is transparent, any colors layered on at this point will mix with the under-lying shades. Here, using a yellow-brown, she defines the rows of kernels on each corn cob.

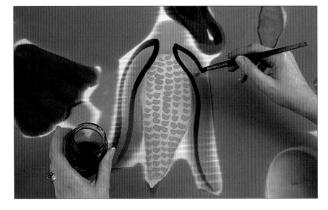

7 Using a dry brush and moss green dye, apply delicate outline strokes to the foliage. Purple strokes are applied around the eggplant and pepper.

8 Using a different, even drier brush with a finer tip, add a second layer of outlining to the foliage with a deep green-black blend.

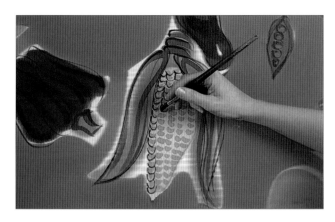

9 The final layer of outlining is added with a charcoal-brown dye.

10 Cathcart does not like to sign her name to her work. Her only "signature" detail is the use of calligraphic-style wording along with the images she paints. Here, using a dry brush, she adds whimsical expressions around the edges of the silk.

11 While this silk is drying, Cathcart moves to another table, spreads a layer of newsprint paper onto a finished piece of silk, and rolls it onto a tube. The silk will be steamed for 90 minutes.

12 The finished product.

David Hartge

David and Linda France
Hartge/Kaleidosilk
Lorikeets, *detail of framed silk*

David Hartge

David and Linda France Hartge/Kaleidosilk
Orchid *square scarf*

MARIANNA HAMILTON ROSS
Autumn Sea Grapes, *36" x 48" silk*

KYMBERLY HENSON
Sleep You Dreamers, *Raw silk reversible coat hand-painted with thickened dyes and pigments*

MARIANNA HAMILTON ROSS
Red Dawn, *36" x 48" silk*

JUDITH BIRD
Hand-dyed and printed silk and rayon kimono

JUDITH BIRD
Crazy Game, *detail*

JUDITH BIRD
Baltimore Painted Screens, *detail*

MICHELLE MARCUSE
45" x 45" Silk jacquard painted with multiple layers of fiber-reactive dyes and resist

MICHELLE MARCUSE
45" x 78" Silk crepe de chine painted with multiple layers of fiber-reactive dyes and resist

MICHELLE MARCUSE
45" x 45" Silk jacquard painted with multiple layers of fiber-reactive dyes and resists

MARIANNA HAMILTON ROSS
Poppies, *76" x 45" silk*

MARIANNA HAMILTON ROSS
Sandra's Begonias, *77" x 45" silk*

MARIANNA HAMILTON ROSS
Heather's Silk, *30" x 42"*

Art of light

LUCINDA CATHCART
*Silk crepe de chine painted
with Procion® fiber-reactive dye*

Art of light

LUCINDA CATHCART
Hand-painted silk yardage using Procion® fiber-reactive dye

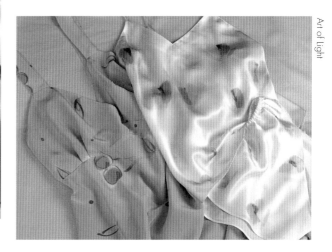

Art of light

LUCINDA CATHCART
*Silk halter dress and camisole painted with
Procion® fiber-reactive dye*

PEGGY RUSSELL/IRO DESIGN
Three scarves, Silk crepe painted with thickened dye

PEGGY RUSSELL/IRO DESIGN
Silk crepe scarf painted with thickened dye

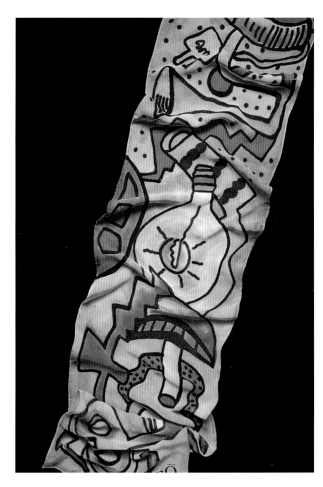

PEGGY RUSSELL/IRO DESIGN
Hand-painted silk

PEGGY RUSSELL/IRO DESIGN
Hand-painted silk

PEGGY RUSSELL/IRO DESIGN
Crepe de chine painted with thickened dye

MARSHALL AND LORI BACIGALUPI/
KISS OF THE WOLF
Hand-painted and quilted silk with salt discharge

MARSHALL AND LORI BACIGALUPI/
KISS OF THE WOLF
Hand-painted and quilted silk with salt discharge

MARSHALL AND LORI BACIGALUPI/
KISS OF THE WOLF
Hand-painted and quilted silk with salt discharge

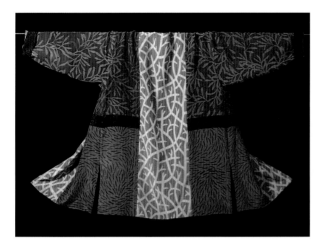

AMY BLACKSTONE
Grove Jacket, *1994, Painted, screen-printed with thickened dye, over-painted with liquid dye*

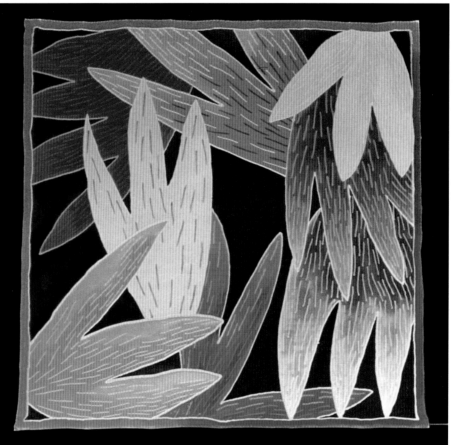

AMY BLACKSTONE
Cactus Scarf, *1990, Inkodye resist and liquid dye*

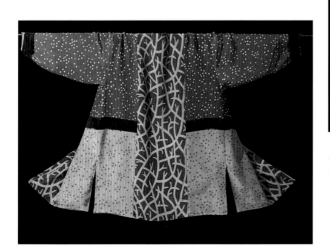

AMY BLACKSTONE
Maple Jacket, *1994, Painted, screen-printed with thickened dye, over-painted with liquid dye*

CHAPTER 4

Tied-Resist Techniques

JUDITH CONTENT
Shibori-*dyed, quilted and appliquéd silk*

Shibori. *Plangi. Chunri.* Tie dye. No matter what term you use, the basic concept for all of these ages-old techniques is the same: String, rope, raffia, rubber bands, clamps, needle and thread, or other devices are used to section off parts of the fabric before dyeing. These barriers "resist" the penetration of the dye and leave unique patterns when they are snipped or untied from the finished product.

Prior to application of the dye, fabric can be finger-dimpled or pulled into knobs, wrapped, and tied. Unusual-shaped objects—rocks, corks, dowels, buttons—can be placed under the fabric before it is tied. Methodical folding before the fabric is tied and dyed results in softly diffuse symmetrical patterns.

Literally thousands of different tied-resist techniques exist; it would require volumes just to elaborate on the many traditional Japanese *shibori* techniques. Because the options are endless, we have chosen to present two lesser-known techniques: a simple and novel variation of traditional *arashi* or *bomaki shibori*; and a series of discharge-and-dye techniques. Both should serve as a launching pad for innovative and experimental techniques of your own making.

Tied-Resist & Discharge

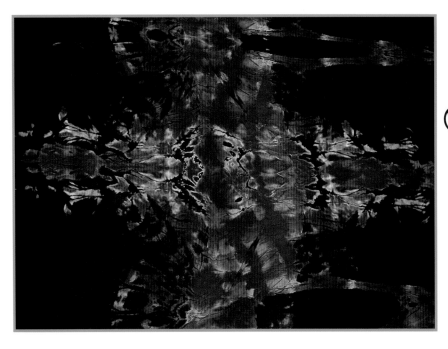

CARTER SMITH
White silk chiffon tied- and injection dyed in multiple applications

He began his career by producing tie-dyed T-shirts while a college student. But although many other children of the 1960s got locked in a Woodstock time warp, Smith evolved to become one of the most inspired and accomplished textile artists of our time.

His brilliant designs—mesmerizing patterns evocative of malachite, tortoise shell, burled wood and butterfly wings—are the by-product of a complex two-step process that combines discharging—a technique that removes color from pre-dyed cloth—and over-dyeing. Prior to dyeing, the cloth is always wrapped, folded, pleated, or puckered into one of several configurations and tightly secured with cord.

Smith is reluctant to package himself, and works out of a secluded, sprawling Victorian home in a small coastal community north of Boston. Even so, his renown as a textile artist and a clothing designer is extensive within the inner circles of the fashion business. His diaphanous bias-cut gowns breathe with life while still on a hanger, and his intricately layered and patterned silks are barely out of the dye bath before they are whisked off to international ports of call and purchased for sums far greater than anyone in the Age of Aquarius ever thought possible. Smith avoids giving names to his techniques. Like him, they defy categorization and are constantly evolving. The only two constants in his techniques are patience and curiosity.

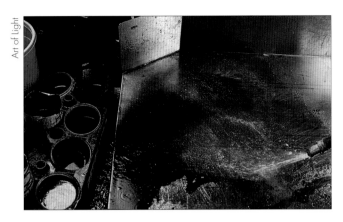

Art of Light

Materials & Equipment:

Silk georgette or chiffon
(approximately 1 ½ yards)

Acid dyes
in your choice of colors

Black acid dye bath
(two non-corrosive pots)

One vegetable steamer

Cotton twine

Bulb baster, tablespoon, or large plastic syringe
(needle removed)

Wooden dowel
approximately 1" (3 cm) in diameter and 20" (60 cm) long

Ironing board and iron

Scissors

Plastic bucket

🍃 *Tip:*

For soft stripes, fold a length of fabric back and forth, accordion-style, into pleats (the tinier the pleats, the more subtle the design will be). Tie off with rubber or string (evenly spaced or not, depending on your preference) and dye.

1 Because much of Smith's work involves immersion dyeing, he prefers to work with acid dyes. He feels that they are less complicated to mix than fiber-reactive dyes, work faster, and require less reliance on the clock. This is important to him because most of his pieces are subjected to numerous rapid-fire dips in the dye and discharge bath. Smith buys his dye in powder form and mixes up stock solutions in advance. He stores them at table-side in open soda-bottle containers that have been cut in half.

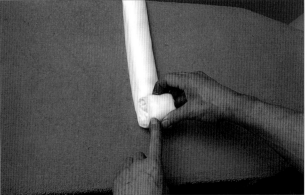

2 Working on your ironing board or a flat work surface, fold a length of silk georgette in half or thirds so that it measures approximately 18 inches (45 cm) wide. Center a 20-inch (48 cm) dowel at one end of the silk and slowly roll the dowel upward until all the silk has been taken up onto the stick. (Folding the material before rolling will help to produce a design with a symmetrical feeling and will enable the color to fade softly in and out of the piece.)

3 Very carefully slide the dowel out of the silk so that the cloth remains rolled. Then, starting at one end, smoothly and firmly roll the tube of silk end-over-end, jelly-roll style.

Rolled & Tied Silk

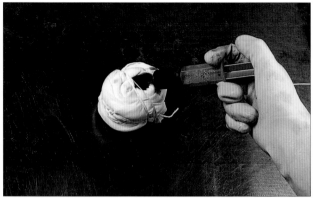

❧ *Tip:*

For a plaid or
windowpane effect,
accordion-pleat the fabric
into a long strip, then
pleat back and forth
again until you have
a square. Tie tightly
vertically and then hori-
zontally before dyeing.

4 Starting at the center, loop nylon twine several times around the roll and pull tightly. Then wrap again so that this series of loops is at right angles to the first. (Rather than knotting, Smith prefers to simply loop and pull on the twine to secure it.)

5 Place the "jelly roll" spiral-side up onto a raised work surface. (Smith uses an old window screen propped up with dowels under two ends. The fine mesh of the screen allows excess dye to drip through and prevents the cloth from sitting in a puddle.) Using a syringe, bulb baster, or a table-spoon, "inject" your first color of dye into the center of the spiral. Because your goal is to control the placement of the dye, do not use a spray bottle or any other device that will cause splattering.

6 Rotate the silk several times and inject several more colors. Use enough dye to thoroughly penetrate the piece, but do not saturate it to the point of dripping. Leave some areas white (these will later be dyed over in a black dye bath.)

7 Generously sprinkle white distilled vinegar (5 percent acidity) all over the rolled cloth. The vinegar provides the acidic medium necessary to activate the dye process.

8 In a non-corrosive stock pot that has been outfitted with a vegetable steamer, bring approximately two inches of water to a boil. Be sure the water does not touch the bottom of the steamer. Place the rolled silk into the steamer basket, cover the pot, and allow to steam for 15 minutes.

9 Remove the silk from the pot and place it under a gentle stream of lukewarm running water. Do not remove the strings at this point. When the water runs clear, gently press the roll to remove some, but not all, of the water. Place the rinsed silk in a non-corrosive pot containing a black acid-dye bath mixed according to manufacturer's instructions for immersion dyeing. Make sure the entire piece is submerged and leave it in the bath for 15 minutes. Stir occasionally.

 Tip:

The amount of water you leave in the wet silk at this point will affect how deeply the next dye bath will penetrate. The more water that remains, the less deep the penetration will be. If you do want the dye bath to penetrate deeply, remove more water by placing the rolled silk in a washing machine and spinning for one to three minutes.

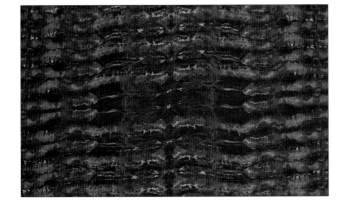

10 Remove the silk from the pot and rinse under warm running water until the water runs clear. Very carefully remove the string, cutting if necessary. (By looping and tugging rather than knotting in the preliminary stages, it is less likely that you will need a scissors to cut the twine.) Wash the finished piece with a mild liquid detergent such as *Synthrapol®*. Dry on medium or low heat until moderately dry and then allow to finish drying at room temperature to protect the serecin in the silk. Gently press with a dry iron.

Materials & Equipment:

All of the items in Technique 1 plus:

Plastic bucket
filled with cold water

Non-corrosive shallow pot
to hold the discharge solution

Sodium hydrosulfite
*(the discharge powder and the active
ingredient in RIT color stripper)
mixed according to directions in approximately
two gallons of water*

Spring-operated clothespins
or other similar clamping devices

The Black Comet

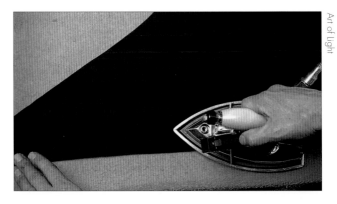

Art of Light

1 Place a square of black silk crepe (chiffon, etc.) diagnally on the work surface so that the corners of the fabric point to north, south, east, and west. An invisible equator runs horizontally from west to east. Grasp the "southern" corner of the silk and bring it up and over toward the east, stopping at the equator. Using an iron outfitted with a scorch guard plate, gently press the fold created along the bottom south-western edge. Next grasp the northern corner and bring it down and over to the right, stopping at the equator. Press. Straighten the folds so that the western corner is cleanly pointed.

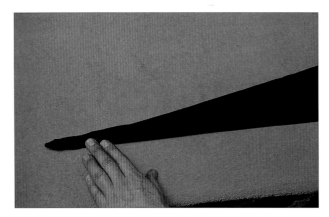

2 The shape you now have before you somewhat resembles a sideways ice-cream cone, with the bottom of the cone pointing to the west. The eastern corner of the cloth (the top of the "ice cream") is a single thickness of fabric; the "cone" portion is a double thickness. Accordion-fold the northern and southern edges of the cone several times, each time bringing the edges to the equator line. Keep the edge sharply pointed and tapered. Press each crease well.

3 The silk now has a very finely tapered point on the left and a wider, fanned-out wedge shape on the right. Place your left hand on the western corner to hold it in place; with your right hand, bring the eastern corner up to the north, forming a right-angle fold.

4 Using a spiral motion, tightly twist the tapered end and coil it inward, jelly-roll style, until it forms a rosette. Be sure to leave the right half of the silk free. This will form the "tail" of the comet. Using the loop-and-tie technique described in step four of Technique One (page 54), secure the rosette.

5 Place the tied silk in a bucket of cold water and allow it to soak for five or ten minutes. The water will act as a resist later when you place the silk in the discharge bath. If you skip this step, the discharge solution will penetrate too far and too quickly into the fabric.

6 Carefully place the wet silk in the discharge bath that is simmering on the stovetop. (The discharge bath can be held in a pan or pot; ideally the container should be big enough to hold the wrapped or tied piece of silk without causing it to buckle. Smith found his tubs at a restaurant supply house.) Take care not to splash the solution, and be sure you are working with plenty of ventilation. The discharge process produces unpleasant and unhealthy fumes.

🌱 *Tip:*

There are a variety of discharge products available, including thiourea dioxide (brand name Thiox®), sodium formaldehyde sulfoxylate (Formusol), and household bleach. Smith prefers sodium hydrosulfite, the generic name for the active ingredient in RIT color stripper, because it works a bit more slowly and gently, giving him the ability to stop anywhere in the discharge process once the cloth has reached a color he likes.

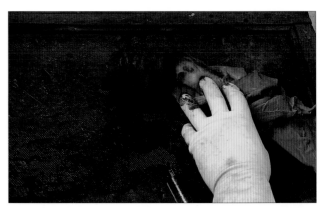

8 When the color has lifted to your satisfaction (it will most likely not turn completely white), remove the silk from the discharge bath and rinse. Do not remove the strings at this point. Gently press the roll to remove some, but not all, of the water.

❦ *Tip:*

For a starburst effect, simply bunch up the fabric and tie string around and around it in a radiating pattern. Wavy, zig-zagged, square, diamond, or other-shaped lines can be created by sewing several folds of fabric together with thick or thin thread and then pulling the thread to gather or bunch the fabric together.

7 Wait and watch as the discharge solution begins to lift the black color from the silk. The cloth will pass through a fascinating spectrum of hues—olive or teal greens, perhaps blue, shades of copper, sepia, umber, and orange—as the black is lifted. While you are waiting, occasionally give the bath a light stir.

9 Place the damp, discharged silk onto a clean, raised mesh work surface and inject dye into the wrapped portion. Work carefully and keep the syringe directly on the fabric as you squeeze. Your goal is not to shoot the dye, which will create spots, but to apply it in an even fashion. Sprinkle distilled white vinegar over the injection-dyed portion.

10 Carefully place the silk onto the steamer basket (see step six on page 57), keeping the "tail" away from the "body" of the fabric. Cover and steam for 15 minutes. (**Note:** Always be sure that the water in the steam pot is boiling before you add the fabric.)

11 Remove from the steam pot and rinse again, leaving the strings intact. Using tongs, lower the tail of the silk into a black dye bath and secure the injection-dyed portion so that it does not fall into the bath. Leave in the dye bath for four to five minutes. This length of exposure should produce a blackish-greenish color around the edges rather than solid black. Variations will occur depending on whether or not the dye bath is boiling and how many other pieces of fabric have been dipped in immediately beforehand.

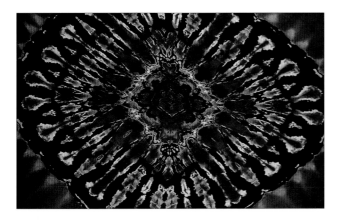 

12 Remove from the dye bath and rinse until the water runs clear. Snip the string carefully and unravel it. Gently open the fabric. Wash the finished piece in the washing machine with a mild liquid detergent such as *Synthrapol*®. Dry on medium or low heat until moderately dry and then remove. Allow to finish drying at room temperature to protect the serecin in the silk.

13 **Variation:** This slide shows a variation of the above technique, in which white silk was used rather than black. After wrapping and tying, the center was injected with dye and steamed (see steps six through nine of Technique one, pages 54 and 55), then overdyed in black for five minutes, and lightly discharged for five minutes prior to rinsing.

Materials & Equipment:

All of the items in Technique 1 and 2 plus:
White silk chiffon or crepe de chine
(instead of black, approximately two yards)

Finger-Pleated Silk

Art of light

1 Wash a length of white silk chiffon and run it through the machine's spin cycle; do not let it dry. Fold it in half or quarters (depending on the size) until you have a moderately-sized square or rectangle. Place the damp fabric directly onto a non-porous work surface (Smith uses stainless-steel tables obtained at a restaurant auction). Using your fingers, press and dimple the fabric. Because it is wet, the fabric will hold the puckers. Be sure the entire surface is dimpled and that the puckers are all relatively the same height.

2 Sandwich the fabric in between the work surface and a flat object such as Plexiglas to keep the fabric weighted down as you tie. Working from left to right, slide a length of string about two inches down from the top of the fabric, loop and pull snugly. Repeat this motion several times, spacing the loops about two inches apart.

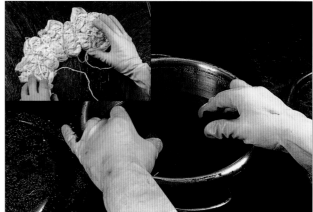

3-4 When the entire piece of silk has been securely tied, bend the silk into a horseshoe shape and tie again, pulling tightest at the tip and slightly looser as you work your way down to the other end.

Submerge the tied silk in a boiling black dye bath for ten to 30 minutes. The longer you leave the fabric in the dye bath, the deeper the black will penetrate into the center of the cloth.

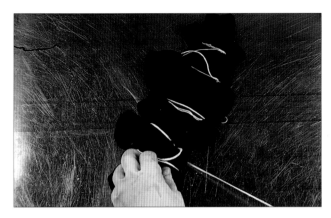

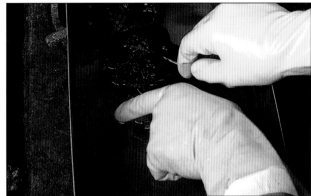

5 Remove the silk from the dye bath and rinse as described in the previous techniques. Do not cut the string yet. Using more cotton cord, tie over the cloth and the first layer of wrapping. Your goal is not to duplicate the path circumscribed by the first wrapping but to intersperse and create a new layer of tied resist.

6 Place the newly tied silk into the discharge bath. This is the first of two dips the cloth will get in the discharge. The first will be longer than the second. Allow the silk to remain there for 15 minutes, or until the color has lifted to your satisfaction.

7 Remove from the discharge bath and rinse. Re-tie the silk again and place in a boiling black dye bath for two to five minutes. Remove from the black dye, rinse, tie over one last time, and discharge again for five minutes or so. The length of time advised for all of these dyeing and discharging steps is somewhat indeterminate and is influenced by many factors: the concentration of your black bath; the strength of the discharge bath; and the temperature of the dye and discharge bath. For best results, the black bath should be boiling but the discharge should be on a slow simmer, around 140-180°F. Otherwise, it will create hot spots that make an uneven pattern.

8 Rinse, carefully untie, and wash as described in step 12 of Technique two.

🌱 *Tip:*

Substitute damp black silk for the white and subject to three separate discharges and three dips in black dye bath, each for less time than the one before it. "The logic for layering is to put a lighter and lighter layer of color on each time," Smith explains. "You start with the long/strong discharge first; keep getting weaker/shorter each time; you can do it five or six times if you want, tying over your black dip, or your discharge, or both, or neither. The goal is to variegate the surface design. If you don't tie anew each time, you may lose some of the layers."

Nouveau Shibori

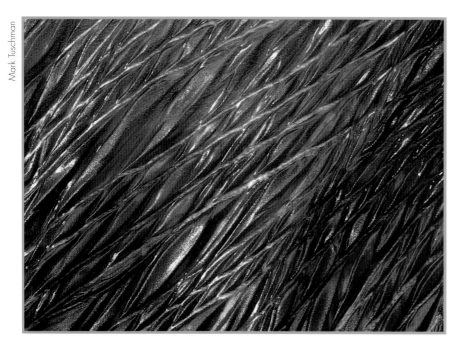

Mark Tuschman

JUDITH CONTENT
Detail, shibori-*dyed, silk satin*

Working from a studio in the heart of California wine country, 37-year-old Judith Content is positive proof that innovation is the heart of successful textile dyeing. After studying traditional Japanese *bomaki shibori* (also called *arashi*) with Ana Lisa Hedstrom, Content devised her own variation of the technique. Rather than wrapping a long wooden pole or PVC pipe with silk, securing with thread, and applying traditional colors such as indigo, Content uses glass wine bottles and very non-traditional color gradations that result from combining turquoise, magenta, and yellow dyes.

After dyeing small pieces of silk, Content then cuts them apart and reassembles the many pieces into quilted, appliquéd panels. The completed pieces range in size from single panels and interpretations of the kimono form, to large-scale, site-specific installations. Her work reflects a deep love of color and the folk art forms of Mexico, Africa, and Asia.

A graduate of San Francisco State University, Judith Content holds a Bachelor of Fine Arts with an emphasis in textiles. She has participated in numerous international exhibitions of *shibori* and surface design, and has been featured in numerous publications. Although constantly refining her *shibori* techniques, Content has also begun to express her fascination with color and fiber by creating hand-painted, resin-coated, and glazed beads from foreign newspapers and kraft paper.

Mark Tuschman

Materials & Equipment:

Large wine or other glass bottle

Pre-washed silk
(the width of the bottle and 24"/62 cm long)

Rubber gloves

String of desired thickness to wrap around bottle
(buttonhole twist thread is used in these photos)

Acid or fiber-reactive dye
diluted to solution

Acetic acid or vinegar
(for acid dye or other recommended setting agent)

Masking tape

Non-corrosive pot for each color used

Hot plates or a stove
to accommodate each dye pot

Long-handled wooden or stainless-steel spoons

Long-handled measuring cup or ladle

1 Assemble your materials. Content uses a granular acid dye that she obtains from a Japanese importer. Along with the fact that its large, weighted granules do not produce air-borne dust when mixed, she likes the dye because it can be activated at lower temperatures than other brands. You can use either acid or fiber-reactive dyes with this technique, she notes. The only thing that would vary would be the process required to set the dye after brief immersions (see step eight).

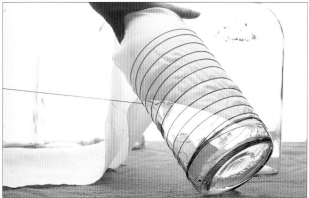

2 With a bit of masking tape, secure the tip of the silk (silk-satin is being used here) to a clear glass bottle. Using buttonhole-twist thread or any type of string desired, wrap the thread around the bottom of the bottle several times, catching in the tip of the fabric. Try to use a length of fabric no more than 24 inches (62 cm) long. If the fabric is much longer, Content explains, it will wrap around the bottle too many times, thus making it difficult for the dye to soak through evenly.

3 Wrap the silk around the bottle, securing it as you go with several rotations of thread. For a symmetrical design, wrap the thread around the bottle at even intervals (the closer together, the finer the dye lines will be in the finished product). If desired, intersperse this wrapping with a second one using a thicker or thinner thread. Secure the thread at the top of the bottle with another bit of masking tape.

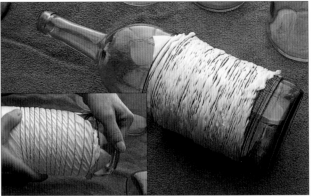

❧ Tip:

*"The wine-bottle technique allows for great range of adaptation,"
Content notes.
For example, you could rainbow-dye a piece of cloth first, let it dry, iron it, and then rewrap the bottle. Discharge by dipping or pouring the solution over the fabric, rinse out the discharge completely, and then either overdye one last time or leave the fabric as is. The effect would be stunning.*

4 Holding the bottle firmly with one hand, use the other hand to gently and firmly twist the silk and push it up toward the top of the bottle. Tiny ripples of pleats will begin to appear.

5 Continue twisting and pushing until the entire piece of silk is pleated. (For an interesting variation, prior to twisting, you might want to leave the top inch of fabric unsecured with thread. After twist-pleating, the top of the fabric will flutter gracefully like the petals of a flower and will thus take up the dye differently than the rest of the fabric.)

6 Holding the bottle by the neck, submerge it in the dye vat. You have several options at this point, depending upon how many colors you are using and how intense you want the coloring to be. If, for example, you want just a blush of color, dip the bottle in as far as you desire and hold it there until you have achieved the shade you like. For a more intense saturation, leave the bottle in the bucket longer. Because an empty bottle will float and bob, you may want to fill it halfway with hot water to keep the bottle submerged to the desired level. If you don't want to dye the entire piece at once, invert a glass bowl of the desired height in the bottom of the bucket, and rest the wrapped bottle on it.

7 Another option for applying the dye is to submerge the bottle upside down, allowing its edge to rest on the lip of your pot or bucket. This will keep the bottle at an angle, thus producing interesting oblique lines in the fabric. "Think in advance about color combinations so that you will know where to dip first," Content advises. "For example, if you dip the whole bottle in yellow first, you could then dip the top in blue to get green, and dip the bottom in red to get orange. It really helps to know some color theory so that you don't end up with some ugly shades."

8 Instead of, or in addition to dipping, the dye can be poured directly over the bottle while it is held over the dye bath. This builds up the color gradually and produces subtle gradations of dyes from several different-colored vats. Content prefers this method. Although the pouring tends to follow the direction of the pleating, it doesn't always go where you want it to, Content warns. Again, using a very small stream of very weak dye gives you more control of the end product.

9 Remove the masking tape from the top and bottom thread. Gently unroll the silk and the thread. The fabric will be delicately pleated. The pleats will stay in the fabric for a long time if the fabric is first dried on the bottle before unwrapping. (They will fall out if the fabric is washed or wet again). Otherwise you can iron them out.) Content prefers to iron things out for a different trademark. (Several *shibori*-ists leave the pleats in as a signature.)

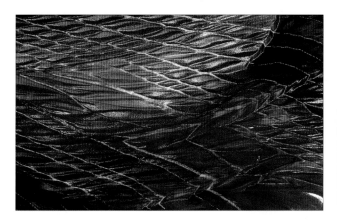

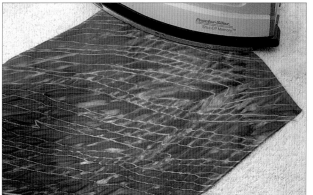

10 Detail shot of the un-ironed, dry silk. Notice the fine white lines that show where the thread resisted the dye. (An interesting variation on this technique would be to use a discharge solution instead of dye, and black or dark-colored cloth instead of white. Wherever you tied the cord, you would end up with a very fine black, rather than white, line.)

11 Iron out the pleats if desired. "Certain *shibori* artists like to leave the pleats in the fabric as part of their signature look," Content explains. "I prefer to press mine completely to allow the dye pattern to emerge and provide texture of its own."

🐛 *Tip:*

Because she favors weak dye solutions and the resulting soft, opalescent shades that come from a short dip (as short as two or three minutes in some cases) in the dye bath, Content sets her dyes by simmering them for 30 to 45 minutes in a bath of water mixed with 98% acetic acid. "This technique works with the type of acid dye I use," she explains. "With different brands, you would probably want to check your manufacturer's instructions."

MICHELLE MARCUSE
*Pin-tucked chiffon,
painted silk*

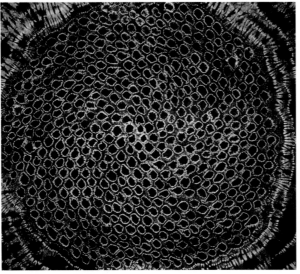

MICHELLE MARCUSE
Pin-tucked chiffon, painted silk

BILLI ROTHOVE
38" x 48" Akete Kano tie dye, acid dye on cotton

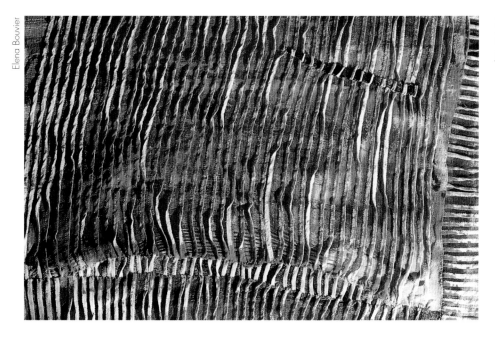

MICHELLE MARCUSE
Did you ever argue with a Buddhist?, *Pin-tucked chiffon, fiber-reactive dyes, sodium alginate, collage*

Elena Bouvier

MICHELLE MARCUSE
Silk chiffon stitched and painted with multiple layers of fiber-reactive dyes and sodium alginate

Elena Bouvier

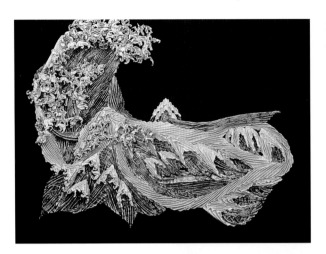

NANETTE DAVIS-SHAKLHO
Homage to Hokusai, 5' x 6' *Arashi* shibori-*dyed silk*

NANETTE DAVIS-SHAKLHO
Skywomb, detail, 1'9" x 3'9" x 8" *Arashi* shibori-*dyed silk*
on wire screen

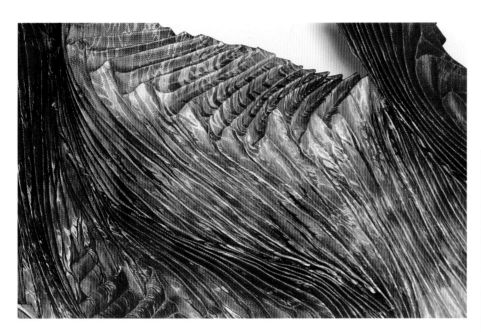

NANETTE DAVIS-SHAKLHO
Alaskan Sunrise, *detail, Arashi* shibori-*dyed silk sculpture*

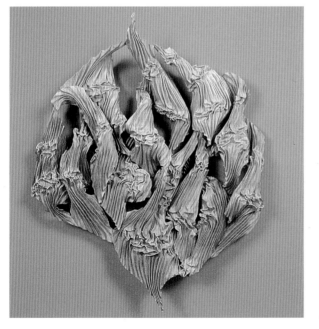

NANETTE DAVIS SHAKLHO
Fire Lotus, *5' x 3' Arashi* shibori-*dyed silk and metal sculpture*

NANETTE DAVIS-SHAKLHO
House of Light, *3'5" x 3'5"* shibori-*dyed silk on wire screen*

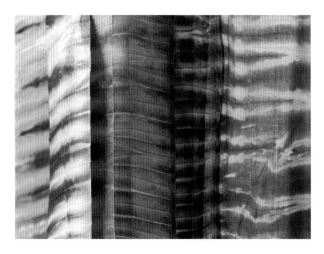

LAURIE GUNDERSON AND MICHAEL DAVIS
Shibori-*dyed silk*

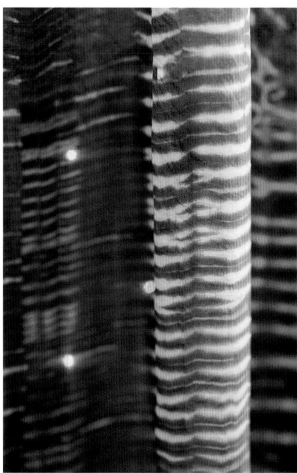

LAURIE GUNDERSON AND MICHAEL DAVIS
Shibori-*dyed silk*

LAURIE GUNDERSON AND MICHAEL DAVIS
Shibori-*dyed silk*

LAURIE GUNDERSON AND MICHAEL DAVIS
Shibori-*dyed silk*

LAURIE GUNDERSON AND MICHAEL DAVIS
Shibori-*dyed yardage*

LAURIE GUNDERSON AND MICHAEL DAVIS
Shibori-*dyed and woven silks*

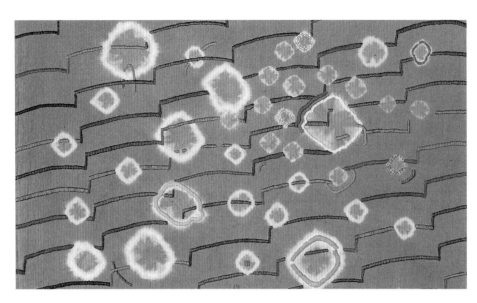

ANNE McKENZIE NICKOLSON
Smoke Rings, *detail, 17 ³/₄" x 18 ¹/₄" Embroidery on*
tie-dyed cotton

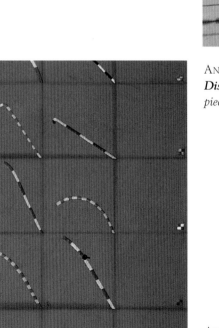

ANNE McKENZIE NICKOLSON
Disjoint, *41 ¹/₂" x 38" Embroidery on clamp-resist dyed,*
pieced raw silk

ANNE McKENZIE NICKOLSON
Mismatch, *45" x 31 ¹/₂" Embroidery on clamp-resist dyed,*
pieced cotton

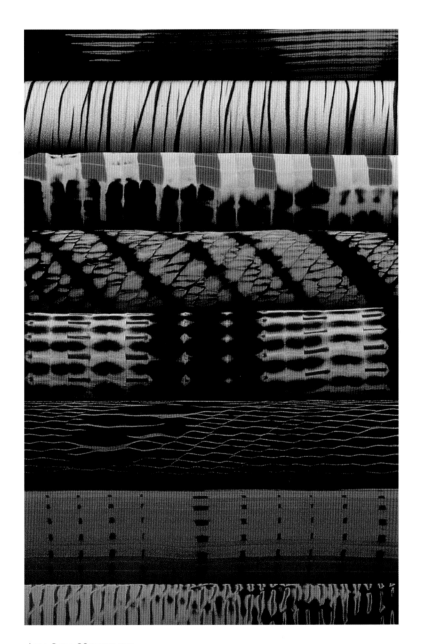

ANA LISA HEDSTROM
Shibori-*dyed silk yardage*

ANA LISA HEDSTROM
Shibori-*dyed and pieced silk jacket*

JUDITH CONTENT
Detail, shibori-*dyed, quilted and appliquéd silk*

JUDITH CONTENT
White Water, *detail,*
6' x 4 1/2 ' shibori-*dyed,*
quilted, appliquéd silk

JUDITH CONTENT
Detail, shibori-*dyed, pieced,*
quilted and appliquéd silk

JUDITH CONTENT
Sweltering Sky kimono, *detail*, shibori-*dyed, pieced silk*

JUDITH CONTENT
Detail, shibori-*dyed, quilted and appliquéd silk*

JUDITH CONTENT
Dragonfly, *detail*, shibori-*dyed, pieced and quilted silk*

CHAPTER 5

Batik Techniques

NOEL DYRENFORTH
Upsurge, 127cm x 95cm, Batik *on cotton*

Just as tie-dye or *shibori* are terms that are used interchangeably to describe one particular technique as well as the entire spectrum of tied-resist methods, the term *batik* is used to describe both a specific and a broad range of techniques that share a common approach.

In its simplest connotation, *batik* is a process in which wax of some sort is melted to liquid consistency, brushed onto the cloth, and used to resist the absorption of dye once the cloth is immersed in or painted with dye. However, wax is not the only substance that can be used as a resist: anything that can go on wet, and dry to a hard, impenetrable barrier—mud, flour paste, even liquid resists such as *gutta* or *Inkodye*—can be employed to create fabrics with a characteristic *batik* flavor. What unifies all of these techniques is the fact that with all *batik* projects, the resist medium is used to coat and cover, rather than simply outline, the area to be resisted.

Although some of the most traditional *batik* work involves a simple monochromatic color scheme—usually indigo on white—the artists featured on these pages show that, where there is persistence and a sense of order, there is no limit to the number of colors that can be used.

Dye

Because control of the wax resist is important in *batik* work, dyes that require a high temperature (such as acid dyes) are not practical. Fiber-reactive and direct dyes are the preferred colorants to use for this technique.

Fabric

While silk seems to be the fiber of choice for so many other dyeing methods, cotton is king (followed close behind by linen) with *batik*. The fiber's durability and resilience after numerous immersions enable it to stand up when protein fibers would begin to weaken.

Waxes & Other Resists

The wax you choose depends on the results you want: a pronounced crackle or veining running through your cloth, or a soft, seamless coloration. There are several different types available, each with varying levels of softness and melting points.

Beeswax is the softest and costliest of the waxes used. It is a mellow yellow color, remains soft after applied to the cloth, and penetrates the fabric well to provide maximum resistance to dye penetration. Although it can be used alone for a smooth, crackle-free design, beeswax is usually mixed with other wax such as paraffin.

Paraffin, a wax made from petroleum, tends to be very brittle after it dries on the cloth. If not applied at a hot enough temperature, it tends to sit on the surface of the cloth and can flake off when handled too much.

Microcrystalline wax is a synthetic beeswax made from petroleum. Usually mixed with paraffin, it can be used for a crackle-free design.

Batik wax is a blend of soft and hard waxes. Some suppliers use a combination of paraffin and beeswax; others use paraffin and microcrystalline. The mix ranges from 25 percent soft wax and 75 percent hard, to a 50-50 blend.

Cold wax, a recent innovation, is a water-soluble resist that does not need to be melted prior to application. It has a lard-like consistency and is applied like a paste. Cold wax tends to sit on the surface of the fabric and tends to erode very quickly. For this reason it is not advised for use with multiple-immersion *batik*.

Other resists. You can create your own paste resists by mixing water with wheat or rice flour, cornstarch, or other starchy substance until you achieve the desired consistency. Experiment with a swatch of cloth first to see how severely the paste flakes off once dry. Because the paste can become messy in a dye bath, direct painting is recommended for use with this kind of resist.

Two-Color *Batik*

Let's say you want to do a simple two-colored project: yellow, white, and green fish in a blue sea. Decide in advance which fish will be yellow, which will be white, and which will be green.

Step 1: After sketching your illustration onto the cloth, wax over any fish you want to remain white. Wet the cloth.

Step 2: Immerse the wet cloth in the yellow dye bath. Remove and let dry.

Step 3: Wax over any of the yellow fish you want to remain yellow. (The wax over the white fish will remain there.)

Step 4: Wet the cloth, immerse it in a pale blue dye bath, remove,

Tools

The **tjanting,** a wooden-handled device with a bulbous metal reservoir at the end, is used by dipping the reservoir into melted wax. The spout that protrudes from the bottom of the reservoir regulates the flow of wax and enables the user to draw lines that range in thickness from fine to broad. *Tjantings* can be purchased in a variety of sizes, including single- and double-spout models.

The **tjap** is a metal printing block that is dipped into a wax-soaked pad (much like an ink-pad) and then pressed into the cloth. It is a convenient tool to use when repeat patterns over a large area of cloth are desired. (Wood can also be carved and used as a *tjap*, although wax will build up in the crevices and will be more difficult to remove than with a metal plate.)

Wood-burning tools, available at hobby stores, are used to solder or melt wax deep into the cloth, or to create surface interest. They usually have a pointed metal end, a wooden handle, and are heated by electricity.

Paintbrushes are used to apply broad fields of wax to the cloth. Use natural-bristle brushes only, as the heat of the wax can cause synthetic bristles to melt.

Scratching tools. By scratching into the waxed surface, you can create interesting surface effects to resemble hair or grass, and geometric patterns such as cross-hatching.

An **electric frying pan** with a thermostat is convenient for melting wax. You can also purchase specially made hot plates designed to melt and hold wax at the ideal temperature. Be advised that the thermostats on most of these devices tend to burn out after a while and render inaccurate readings. Because wax is highly combustible if it exceeds its melting point, use your nose and eyes as a guide: if the wax starts to smell burned and begins to smoke, it is too hot.

An **iron** is used to melt out the waxing after your final dye application is complete. Sandwich your fabric between multiple layers of kraft paper or newsprint (blank only) and press with a hot iron to blot up the wax.

Techniques

Traditional *batik* consists of a single color of dye applied over white cloth. When the wax or other resist is removed, the images remaining will be white and the background will be colored.

If you want to create multiple-colored *batik* work, you must think out the design carefully, select the colors you want to see in finished piece, and determine the sequence you should follow to achieve these colors. Generally, the procedure involves starting with light and warm colors and graduating toward dark, cool colors.

Two-Color *Batik* (cont.)

and hang to dry. Because yellow and blue combine to make green, the unwaxed fish that were yellow from the previous dye bath will now be green. The white and yellow fish remain waxed.

Step 5: Wax over the green fish, wet the cloth, and immerse it in a dark blue dye bath. Remove and let dry. The background—i.e., the water—will be dark blue-green, and your fish will be white, yellow, and green.

Step 6: After drying, remove excess wax by sandwiching the fabric between layers of paper (see the following step-by-step photographs).

Multi-Colored Batik

ARNELLE DOW
38" x 26" **Day Lily,** *Oriental Scroll Series*

From a distance, Arnelle Dow's *batik* masterpieces appear to be watercolor paintings. Closer examination reveals that the shading, depth, and texture of her works are actually the result of repeated applications of wax on cloth.

The Cincinnati, Ohio, artist sometimes adds a few hand-painted images to her *batik* work. However, she is quick to point out that she considers direct painting to be a violation of the Zen purity of *batik*. "A craft like this one has steps you must acknowledge," she explains, "and any color blend you get happens because you have made the effort to go through the necessary steps. If you just paint a color on, the harmony seems to be destroyed."

Dow's works on linen (her preferred fiber) often involve 15 separate immersions in dye. While it may be tedious, the effort is what makes *batik* special to her. "People are very impatient these days to get a result," she says. "Direct application seems to be an offshoot of this impatience. But *batik* done in a traditional manner is not about results; it's about process."

Dow's process involves three key techniques: a progression of dye baths, working from light to dark and warm to cool colors; the use of 50-50 paraffin and beeswax for a softer, crack-free surface; and the use of a wood-burning tool to contour or texture the wax, melt it deeply into the fiber, and "solder" the cracks out of the wax.

80

Tony Walsh

1 After sketching your design onto paper, transfer it onto the fabric. Use a piece of fabric several inches larger than the finished image area and center the design so that several inches of border are on all sides. Using a light table or a brightly lit window, tape the sketch onto the surface and place the fabric on top. Trace the design with an ebony pencil. Ebony is very soft, which allows you to get a nice dark line without pressing hard. It washes out as you dye, leaving no visible marks.

Materials & Equipment:

Fiber-reactive *Procion*® *MX* dye in six colors:
Turquoise, Navy, Golden Yellow, Brilliant/Sun Yellow, Fuschia, and Scarlet.

Additives for fiber-reactive immersion dyeing
as specified by manufacturer (soda ash, salt, Synthrapol®)

Natural bristle, wood-handled brushes
Two-inch-wide, .75-inch-wide, .25-inch-wide

Linen or any medium-weight cellulosic fabric
cut to a square size of your choice

Wood-burning tool

Speedball® pen
(wooden handle with metal nib tip)

Electric skillet to melt wax, set at 280°F

Clothes pins, synthetic clothesline

Light table or window

Tape, dye tubs, iron

Newsprint or kraft paper

2 Place a 50-50 blend of beeswax and paraffin in an electric skillet located in a well-ventilated area. Melt the wax and heat it until the temperature reaches approximately 250°F. Do not let the wax smoke, which indicates it is too hot.

Using a natural-bristle brush, wax over any area you want to remain white/natural-colored in the finished product.

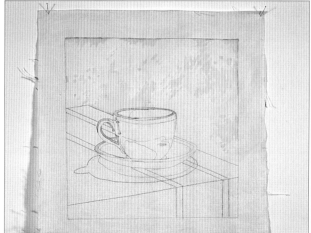

3 When you first apply the wax, it will be two times darker than it will be after drying. To make sure that you have thoroughly saturated the fabric with wax, hold the fabric up to a light source or over a light table.

Tip:

To create a color key that will record the first and each of the subsequent immersions, place a 1/4-inch-wide streak of wax in the right-hand margin outside of the image area. When your dyeing is completely finished, you can trim away this margin and use it as a reference for future projects. Clip the strip to an index card and write down any notations regarding the formulas used for each dye color.

5 After immersion and drying, the waxed fabric is now an overall cream color. Note the dark cream-colored "key" on the upper right edge of the cloth. This number of color swatches on the key will increase with subsequent immersions.

4 Prepare a cream-colored dyebath (if mixing from powder, a touch of scarlet and fuschia blended with yellow) and immerse the waxed cloth. If using *Procion*® *MX* fiber-reactive dyes, Dow's recommended procedure is as follows: A. Wet the waxed fabric in clear water and hang it to remove excess water. Do not let it dry out completely. B. Add liquid dye solution and salt to water in the dye tub and stir well. C. Immerse fabric and agitate to keep fabric completely submerged. D. Remove fabric and add soda ash to the dye bath as suggested by manufacturer. E. Return fabric, agitate for ten minutes, and dispose of dye. F. Hang fabric for 30 minutes minimum to allow dye to bond onto fabric. G. Rinse in cool water till it runs clear, then in warm water, and then soak in water and *Synthrapol*® Rinse and hang to dry. These steps will be repeated each time the fabric is immersed in a new color.

6 Wax over the areas you wish to remain cream-colored. For the color key, place a second streak of wax in the margin next to the first one.

8 Hang the dyed fabric to dry. Any unwaxed area that was cream will now be a taupe color.

7 Wet the fabric, allow the excess to drip out, and immerse the damp fabric in a pale violet-tinted bath (if mixing from powder, a combination of fuchsia and turquoise). Follow step four and the manufacturer's instructions for immersion dyeing and rinsing.

9 Wax over areas you want to remain taupe. Remember that your backgrounds and surfaces will be more interesting if they feature gradations of color, so be sure to wax over *patches* of key areas, rather than a solid field, to allow them to take on coloration from several different immersions. For the color key, place a 1/4-inch-wide streak of wax in the margin directly to the right of the first two (see step six).

Tip:

By using a synthetic clothesline, you will not have to worry about dye bleeding from your fabric onto the rope as it hangs. Before hanging subsequent pieces of fabric, wipe down the clothesline with a clean dry cloth.

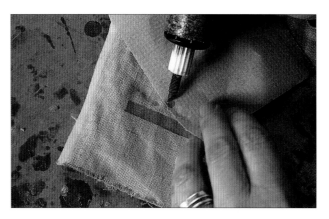

10 If there are any places on the fabric where unwanted blobs of wax have fallen, you can remove them with a wood-burning tool. Place several layers of towelling on a surface, then place the fabric face-up, and cover the blobs with a single piece of towelling. Apply the wood-burning tool to blot up the wax. Keep moving the towel around to find a clean space until all the wax is out. When ready to immerse in the dye bath, rub a little plain liquid soap onto the wet fabric on both sides of the spot you are trying to remove.

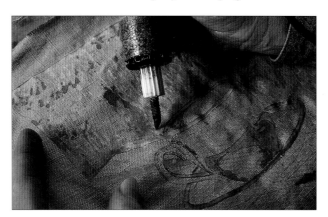

11 To create a softly color-washed, mottled effect in desired areas (for example, on the cup), vary the thickness of the wax by using a wood-burning tool to thin and melt it deep into the fiber of the cloth. (When the wax is thick, it blocks dye more. When the wax is thin, the surface of the cloth continues to dye somewhat.) Some areas of wax may be so thin that they simply look like grease spots.

12 Wet the fabric, allow the excess to drip out, and immerse the damp fabric in a golden-yellow dye bath. Follow step four and the manufacturer's instructions for immersion dyeing and rinsing. Hang to dry. Any unwaxed areas that were mauve will now be golden yellow.

13 Wax over any areas you wish to remain golden yellow. For the color key, place a 1/4-inch-wide streak of wax in the margin directly to the right of the first three (see step six). Double-wax in the highlight area of the saucer (and in any areas you want to have the purest, most vivid color). To double-wax, apply one layer on the front of the fabric, a second layer on the reverse side, and a final application on the front again. Look through light source to ensure saturation.

14 Wet the fabric, allow the excess to drip out, and immerse the damp fabric in a medium turquoise tint. Follow step four and the manufacturer's instructions for immersion dyeing and rinsing. Hang to dry. Any unwaxed areas that were golden yellow will now be a sage green. Allow to dry.

16 Wet the fabric, allow the excess to drip out, and immerse the damp fabric in a violet/rose dye bath (a blend of turquoise and fuchsia). Follow step four and the manufacturer's instructions for immersion dyeing and rinsing. Hang to dry. Any unwaxed areas that were green will now be dusty purple. Allow to dry.

15 Wax over any areas you wish to remain sage green. For the color key, place a 1/4-inch-wide streak of wax in the margin directly to the right of the first four (see step six).

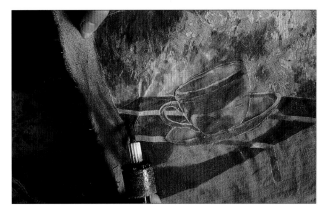

17 Here, and at any other point along the way, seal any waxed areas that have begun to crack from repeated dye baths by applying the wood-burning tool. Seal on both sides of the cloth.

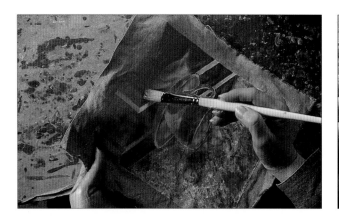

18 Wax over any areas you wish to remain dusty purple. For the color key, place a 1/4-inch-wide streak of wax in the margin directly to the right of the first five (see step six). Again, look through a light source to make sure the wax has penetrated the cloth completely.

20 Wax over areas you want to remain gray-blue. For the color key, place a 1/4-inch-wide streak of wax in the margin directly to the right of the first six (see step six). Using a sharp, pointed tool such as the tip of a compass, a crewel needle, etc, a signature may be carved into the wax. This technique, called *sgraffito*, is ideal if you want to create textures for hair, grasses, etc. Dow prefers to use sharp tools such as this, and a Ukranian Easter-egg tool called a *kistka*, instead of *tjantings* for her fine detail work.

19 Wet the fabric, allow the excess to drip out, and immerse the damp fabric in a light-teal dyebath. (When mixed from scratch, teal usually has a bit of red mixed in with turquoise/navy/lemon. But since there is already red in the cloth, you can leave it out of the dye mix.) Follow step four and the manufacturer's instructions for immersion dyeing and rinsing. Hang to dry. Any unwaxed areas that were dusty purple will now be a gray-blue.

21 Wet the fabric, allow the excess to drip out, and immerse the damp fabric in a dark-blue dye bath (navy, turquoise, lemon, and scarlet). Follow step four and the manufacturer's instructions for immersion dyeing and rinsing. Hang to dry. Any unwaxed areas that were gray-blue will now be a dark, rich midnight blue.

22 Wax over any areas you wish to remain midnight blue. For the color key, place a 1/4-inch-wide streak of wax in the margin directly to the right of the first seven (see step six).Use the wood-burning tool to seal any cracks in the wax. Wet the fabric, allow the excess to drip out, and immerse the damp fabric in a dark teal-green dye bath (add more yellow to the dark navy formula; don't re-use the dye bath!). Follow step four and the manufacturer's instructions for immersion dyeing and rinsing. Hang to dry. Unwaxed areas that were midnight blue will now be a deep, grayed teal.

24 When you have removed as much wax as possible, send the fabric to the dry cleaner to have the final residue of wax removed. (This can also be done at home by boiling the fabric and skimming the water, or by applying paint thinner. Both options are messy, time-consuming, and can produce noxious fumes. A dry cleaner is better-equipped to rid the fabric of the excess wax.)

23 After the fabric has dried and cured, iron the wax out of the fabric. Sandwich the fabric face-up between many thicknesses of blank newsprint paper. Apply direct downward pressure with a hot iron—do not slide the iron around—and blot up the excess wax. You will need to reposition the paper several times and perhaps even replace it with clean paper to ensure that as much wax as possible is blotted.

Tip:

Multi-colored Batik *work requires great planning and an intimate knowledge of color mixing. See Chapter 8 for basic color theory and for suggestions on where to turn for more in-depth guidelines on layering color upon color.*

ARNELLE DOW
Fence Post, detail

ARNELLE DOW
Tiger Lilies, 20" x 16"

ARNELLE DOW
18" x 26" Batik *on linen*

ARNELLE DOW
Mixed Media, *18" x 28"* Batik *with fabric paint*

ARNELLE DOW
Mixed Media, *28" x 40"* Batik *with fabric paint*

ARNELLE DOW
28" x 40" Batik *with fabric paint*

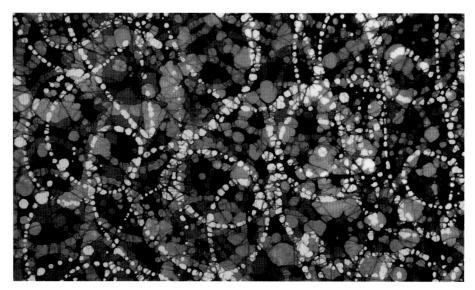

BILLI R.S. ROTHOVE
18" x 18" Candlewax on cotton

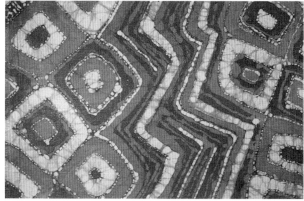

BILLI R.S. ROTHOVE
13" x 21" placemat, Candlewax on linen

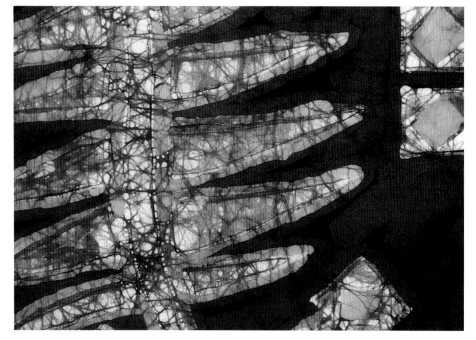

BILLI R.S. ROTHOVE
18" x 18" Candlewax on cotton

BILLI R.S. ROTHOVE
Detail, 16" x 36" Candlewax on cotton

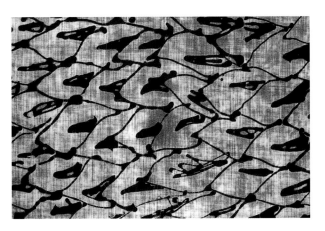

BILLI R.S. ROTHOVE
12" x 20" Candlewax on black cotton, bleach discharge

BILLI R.S. ROTHOVE
22" x 32" Paraffin and beeswax on cotton

JOSEPH ALMYDA
Batik *on Silk*

JOSEPH ALMYDA
Batik *on Silk*

JOSEPH ALMYDA
Batik *on Silk*

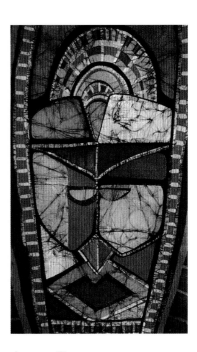

ASTRITH DEYRUP
Mask

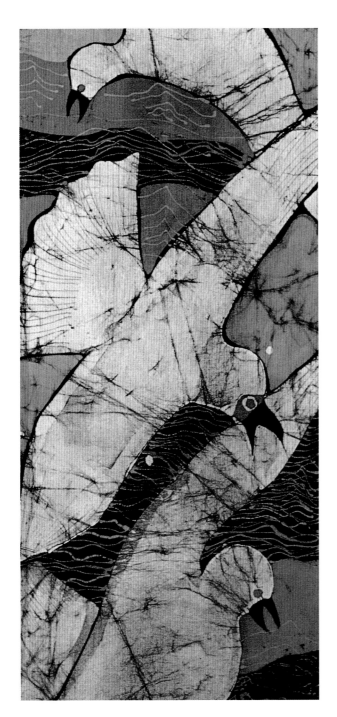

ASTRITH DEYRUP
Mask

ASTRITH DEYRUP
Seagulls

NOEL DYRENFORTH
Upstart, *127 x 95cm*

NOEL DYRENFORTH
Approach, *56 x 56 x 94cm Silk* batik

NOEL DYRENFORTH
Edge, *127 x 95cm* Batik *on cotton*

VIGGO HOLM MADSEN
Cat in a Box, Batik

VIGGO HOLM MADSEN
Juicy Tomato, Batik *on silk*

VIGGO HOLM MADSEN
The Ark

CHAPTER 6

Block Printing

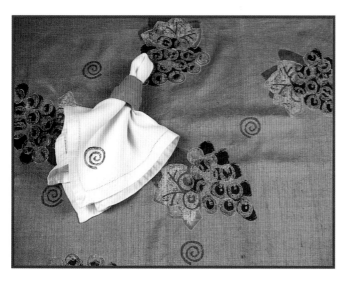

LUCINDA CATHCART
*Thai silk, hand-painted with fiber-reative dye,
stamped with gold pigment*

Wood blocks, linoleum, and rubber stamps provide a welcome change of pace for textile artists who are accustomed to hand-painting every single motif on a piece of cloth. But, along with introducing an element of speed and uniformity to a work, they can also add whimsy, intrigue, and dimension—especially when used in combination with one of the other techniques discussed in this book.

The general principle behind block printing is simple: Draw a design on a solid block of wood, rubber, Styrofoam—yes, even the proverbial potato—carve out the unwanted areas to create a raised, patterned surface, apply the coloring medium, and invert the block onto the fabric.

Today, more and more artists are gravitating to pigments for printing applications. But by combining fiber-reactive dyes with a thickening agent such as sodium alginate, it is possible to get great results with the added benefits that come from using dyes: transparent color layering, a softer hand, and greater permanence.

You can cut your own blocks or use ready-made stamps. If using the latter, bear in mind that stamps designed for use on paper are often too deeply cut for all of their details to transfer onto fabric. Stamps specially designed for fabric are recommended. When working with blocks, remember that your design must be drawn in reverse so that it will appear right-side up when you print.

Prints made with wood, rubber, and linoleum all have their own subtle differences. Wood, because it is harder to contour than linoleum, creates a rustic, choppy effect. Linoleum is easier to carve and lends itself to more detailed designs. Thin sheets of rubber can be cut out in intricate shapes—snowflakes, lace patterns, and undulating forms—with scissors, rather than with cumbersome wood-cutting tools. Both rubber and linoleum are ideal for applying several colors on the same block before inverting it.

Blocks and stamps are effective tools for applying resists, such as wax, to cloth. Spread out your pre-washed cloth, and apply a resist to your block. Quickly press the block onto the cloth in the desired configuration while the wax is still hot, and then dye or discharge as desired. Canadian artist Dorothy Caldwell uses this method masterfully in her intricate wall hangings (see showcase).

Finally, don't overlook the possibility of negative resist printing instead of, or in combination with, block printing. Lay a number of items—feathers, leaves, hand-cut stencil shapes, and so forth—on top of your fabric in a random or symmetrical arrangement. Next, ink a large or small paint roller with thickened dye. Roll directly over the loose shapes and then gently remove them. The background of the cloth will be colored and the image area will be white.

LUCINDA CATHCART
Cotton t-shirts, linoleum block-printed with dyes, discharge, and metallic pigment

Lucinda Cathcart

Lucinda Cathcart, whose watercolored silks were featured in Chapter 3, often uses block-printed motifs on the upholstery fabric she custom designs for her northern Massachusetts clientele. She provided the instructions for the step-by-step technique that follows.

Art of Light

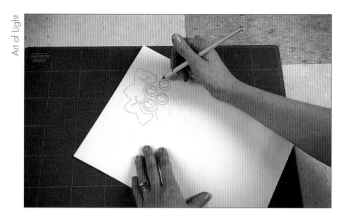

1 Using tracing paper and a soft lead pencil, make a rough sketch of your design. Refine the sketch and fill in detail to make it more graphic. In terms of block printing, keep in mind that you aren't looking for representational perfection but rather the suggestion of shapes and shadows.

Materials & Equipment:

Cardboard
Tracing paper
Soft lead pencils
Masking tape
Art knife or sharp scissors
Two-sided linoleum printing blocks
Wood- or linoleum-cutting tools
Fiber-reactive dye
(thickened with sodium alginate)
Gold metallic pigment
(optional)
Your choice of fabric
(Thai silk is used here)
Flat-headed stencil brushes
(in assorted sizes)

2 Using the soft lead pencil, heavily shade in the areas that will be inked on the block. Don't forget that if you are going to include lettering, it must be drawn in reverse on paper so that it will print right-side up.

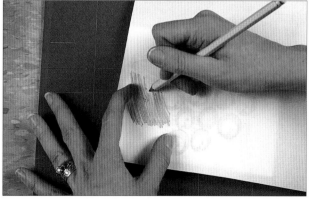

3 Place the penciled-in sketch face down on top of a piece of linoleum (Cathcart uses *Speedy Cut®* two-sided printing blocks, which are available at most art-supply stores). Rub firmly with the handle of a spoon, a burnishing tool, or the edge of a pencil to transfer the design onto the block.

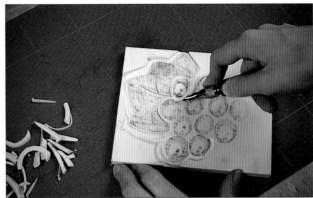

4 Carefully peel back a portion of the sketch halfway through the process to make sure the transfer is taking place. You may need to rub the surface several times to completely transfer your design. (As an alternative to this technique, you can place carbon paper or dressmaker's carbon face down on the block and place your sketch face up. Then simply trace directly over your design completely.)

5 Using wood- or linoleum-carving tools, carve away the portions of the block that you do not want to print. Remember that any raised area will print, so make sure you either clean up the block carefully or texture the background surfaces so that the primary image stands out.

6 To give dimension to this piece, the stamped images will be combined with hand-painted ones. To make a guide for the placement of the hand-painted images, cut an outline template out of cardboard using your original sketch. Place the template on the fabric (depending on the size, it may need to be secured with bits of tape). Using a flat-headed brush, firmly dip the brush into a small amount of thickened dye. Press the dye into the brush using a rotating motion. Use a similar rubbing/rotating motion to push the dye into the cloth.

7 Pour a small amount of a dye in a saucer and dip a flat-headed stencil brush into it, then dab thickened dye onto one of the blocks. Do this carefully to prevent excess dye from accumulating in the crevices. Be sure not to get dye on the surrounding parts of the block, or it will leave an unwanted outline on your cloth.

8 Carefully invert the block onto the fabric and use a burnishing tool to firmly transfer the design.

9 Lift the block up slowly to prevent smearing. Repeat steps seven through nine as needed for each different graphic you create.

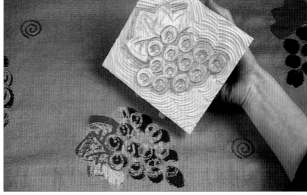

10 After the secondary motifs are applied, ink the primary block. Thickened dyes may be used, but for the sake of contrast and an extra bit of textural interest, a metallic pigment was chosen for this piece. Although you do not want it dripping off the edges, it is important to apply the dye or pigment in several steps, building it up in layers. You will need to re-ink the block after each application, but after a while the layering described in the previous sentence will not be as necessary.

11 For a whimsical touch, place the block off-register using the hand-painted images as a rough guide. Roll to burnish it well and gently peel away. The fabric may adhere in places as you pull the block up.

Allow the finished piece to cure for the proper amount of time. If pigments are used along with the fiber-reactive dye, be sure to factor in their curing time, too. "Some pigments need 24 hours to cure," Cathcart notes; "others can be set with an iron."

DOROTHY CALDWELL
Hole in the Sky, *Wax resist (applied with hand-carved block) and discharge, acrylic on 4' x 4' cotton*

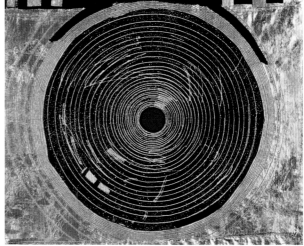

DOROTHY CALDWELL
Will the Moon always be there?, *Wax resist (applied with hand-carved block) and discharge, stitching, appliqué and goldleaf on 18" x 22" cotton*

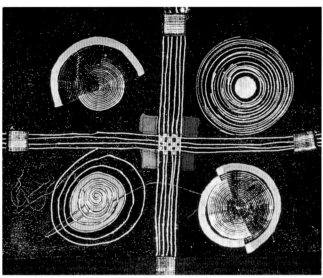

DOROTHY CALDWELL
Is this the same Moon as before?, *Wax resist (applied with hand-carved block) and discharge, appliqué, stitching, and goldleaf on 18" x 22" cotton*

DOROTHY CALDWELL
Landstat, *detail, Wax resist (applied with hand-carved block) and discharge, appliqué, acrylic, goldleaf, and quilting on 20" x 50" cotton*

JEANNE ADAMS
Silk scarf, *Linoleum-block-printed with dyes, discharge, and metallic pigment*

JEANNE ADAMS
Silk scarf, *Linoleum-block-printed with dyes, discharge, and metallic pigment*

JEANNE ADAMS
Silk scarf, *Linoleum-block-printed with dyes, discharge, and metallic pigment*

JEANNE ADAMS
Silk scarf, *Linoleum-block-printed with dyes, discharge, and metallic pigment*

JEANNE ADAMS
Silk scarf, *Linoleum-block-printed with dyes,*
discharge, and metallic pigment

JEANNE ADAMS
Silk tank dress, *Linoleum-block-printed with dyes,*
discharge, and pigment

JEANNE ADAMS
Silk tunic vest, *Linoleum-block-printed with dyes,*
discharge, and metallic pigment

JEANNE ADAMS
Silk tank dress, *Linoleum-block-printed with dyes,*
discharge, and pigment

CHAPTER 7

Marbling Techniques

P.B. Schad
Over-marbling with zig-zag pattern

Although done for centuries on paper, marbling on fabric has become wildly popular in recent years, due in part to the availability of new materials that make it possible for the coloring medium to adhere to cloth.

There are a number of preliminary steps necessary to ensure a successful result. The following preparation should be done the day before you plan to marble.

Preliminary Set-Up

Mix the size. In order for the colorant to sit on the surface of the water, the water needs to be combined with a substance called a "size." The two most commonly used sizes are carrageenan and methyl cellulose. Sizes are mixed with water, one small batch at a time, and then left to sit overnight to make sure that all air bubbles in the mixture have been released. If not, blank spaces will show up in your pattern. Because the temperature of the size can affect how well the paint spreads, be sure to work in a room that is neither too hot nor too cold. Room temperature is best.

Mix the paint to the proper consistency (see test sample, below) and put in applicator bottles. You can use slightly thickened dyes, pre-mixed pigments that are already the correct consistency for marbling (e.g., *Deka Permanent* or *Perm-Air, Pebeo,* or *PAOfah*), or any other paint product. Water-based acrylic paints allow for the easiest clean-up.

Make a test sample and observe the following:
Did the paint sink? If so, it is too heavy. Thin it slightly with a drop or two of distilled water. If the paint won't spread or has jagged edges, the size may be too thick. Thin it with distilled water and try again. Each drop of paint should not spread beyond two to three inches in diameter. If the paint spreads too far, it is too thin.

Prepare the fabric. As with dyeing, fabric for marbling needs to be washed to remove all sizing, linters, etc. But for marbling, it also needs to be pre-treated with aluminum sulfate (alum). This helps provide the "charge" that draws and holds the pigment onto the fabric. Use about 1/4 cup of alum per gallon of water and soak at least 30 minutes in the alum. Wring well, hang to dry, then iron the fabric *flat*. Do not fold it or else the wrinkles will not take up the pattern.

Tools and Equipment

The most important tool in your marbling arsenal is the tray or tub used to hold your size. It must be wide enough to accommodate the fully unfurled piece of fabric you plan to marble, and it must be deep enough to hold the size. Few marbling projects require the size to be filled to a depth of more than two inches, so avoid using tubs deeper than that. Otherwise, it will be difficult for you to lean over and apply the dyes.

Anything you can find or build will work for a tub. Featured artist Laura Crandall uses aluminum tanks that she had a welder fabricate for her. Beginners often use photographic trays or dish pans.

There are literally hundreds of different patterns you can create when marbling. Each is created by using different tools and by swirling, dragging, or combing in a variety of directions.

For small projects, you can use bamboo skewers, hair picks, metal combs, or knitting needles. Larger rakes can be made by hammering nails evenly across a thin piece of lumber cut to fit the length of your tub, or by drilling holes and inserting objects such as golf tees, dowels, etc.

General Techniques

Marbling patterns are created by dragging various tools across the surface of the tub.

There are two ways to add color: **(1)** in between each other, or **(2)** on top of each other. Remember that when you add colors to the tub, they will not mix together but will either sit on top of each other or squeeze each other out.

Once you drop the colors onto the size, you can swirl or drag through them to create any of the following:

Hearts: Drop circles of different sizes. Drag a skewer or knitting needle through the center from top to bottom.

Stones: Just drop different sizes and colors of paint next to each other. They will squeeze next to each other in amoeba-like shapes, the more you add.

Free form: Use a feather, skewer, or other pointed object to casually swirl through the entire vat of color. *Que sera sera!*

Arcs: Using the rake, pull from top to bottom. Leave as is or drag again at right angles.

Feathers: Do as above, but then reposition the rake (see following technique).

Try This On For Size

Carrageenan and methyl cellulose—the two primary sizes used in marbling—each have their advocates. Methyl cellulose has a longer life than carrageenan, which is only good for a couple of days, and does not require advance preparation. "Many people who work on a small scale like the fact that with methyl cellulose you don't have to wait; it's ready in a half hour." In spite of the convenience, however, Crandall prefers to use carrageenan for her projects. "I like the way it holds the paint," she explains, "but I've been working with it so long I know how to read it. Beginners may want to start first with methyl cellulose and then switch over to carrageenan to compare results."

LAURA CRANDALL
Assorted men's ties, marbled silk

Marbling

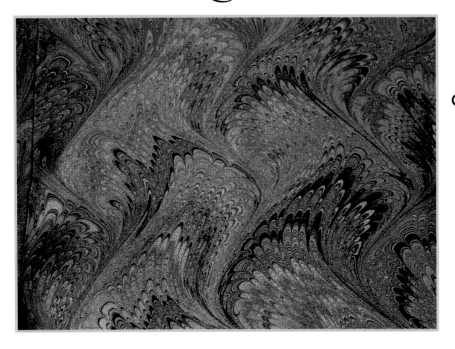

LAURA CRANDALL
Detail, marbled silk

*L*aura Crandall's love affair with textiles began in college, first *batiking* t-shirts and then moving on to screen-type printing. But it wasn't until fifteen years ago, during a trip to Italy, that she found her true calling.

"I was in Florence, the world center for fine marbled papers, and everywhere I looked the stores were full of it: pencils, stationery, books," she recalls. "I fell totally in love with it." There were no books available on marbling fabric, so she developed her own technique. "I found and made all the tools myself by trial and error," she adds. "I wasted a lot of money on things that didn't work. But since I have scientists for parents, the experimentation gene was always there and I didn't give up."

Today, Crandall's Marbled Masterpieces are hot sellers at specialty shops throughout the country. However, she prefers to sell primarily at craft fairs. "I truly enjoy getting a chance to meet my customers and get their feedback," she explains. "We artists always hate everything we do, so it's a real restorative to hear someone saying, 'Gee, this is beautiful!'"

Crandall likes to work on dark-color fabrics using opaque paints rather than translucent dyes. "The more opaque a paint is," she explains, "the more true it will be on a darker color." Always, though, there is the element of surprise. "There is a lot about this process I control," says Crandall the scientist. "And a lot," adds Crandall the artist, "I just leave up to the marbling muse."

112

Materials & Equipment:

Iridescent silver paint
Iridescent gold paint
Iridescent pink paint
Red paint
Black paint
Carrageenan or methyl cellulose size
Combs and rakes
Fabric
Tub
wide enough to hold the entire unfolded fabric

1 Fill the tub with carrageenan solution (see page 110 for instructions) or methyl cellulose to a depth of one or two inches. (If you use less size, the paint is easier to control but won't flow as delicately. You want it to flow if you plan to do finely combed patterns.) Then begin to apply your first colors. Here, a shiny pink is being dropped on top of a very light amount of silver. Add the pigment drop by drop with dropper bottles containing paints thinned down to desired consistency.

"Each person finds a paint that works for them and a thickness," Crandall explains. "The ideal thickness depends a lot on the depth of the size in your tub. The thicker the paint, the more it will spread (although if it's too thick it will just drop to the bottom of the pan. But if it's very thick, it just pushes and pushes and keeps expanding, so you have to find your own happy medium.) It is best to pre-test in a small amount of carrageenan in a small bowl."

2 Crandall's third color—red—is applied in the same way. "When applying the paint," says Crandall, "keep your hand close to the surface of the size. The closer you are to the tank, the less time it takes for the drop to hit the vat." Don't drop too much, or too fast, or the paint will splatter.

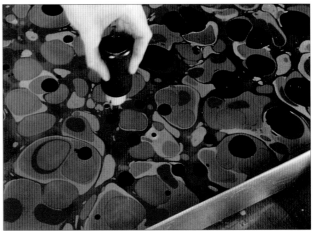

3 The fourth color, an iridescent gold, is added on top of the silver, pink, and red. The quantity of each, says Crandall, is totally subjective.

4 The final color, black, is added. Does it matter which color you put down first? It can. "The color you put down first will be the color that shows up least in the final product," Crandall explains, "because it gets squeezed into smaller and smaller areas by the successive colors. For example, I like black and wanted to make sure there was enough black in the fabric, so I put this color on last."

5 After the final color is applied, wait for several minutes for the colors to spread. Although the drops begin small, they will increase in size for several minutes. "They will eventually stop moving," Crandall says. "But you have to be sure to wait until it looks like things have completely stopped." At this stage in the process, the multi-colored solution now in the tank is called a *get-gel*.

6 Using a tool called a *rake*, Laura and her assistant place the bar over the frame and carefully drag from top to bottom. The rake is a piece of wood whose "teeth" are pieces of 1/4-inch diameter dowel inserted every three inches. The teeth are long enough that they stick into the tank about halfway into the size, just deep enough to drag the surface.

7 When they reach the opposite side of the tank, they gently raise the rake and reposition it about 1 1/2 inches to the left or right so that the teeth straddle the places where they originally were. The rake is now pulled back up, from bottom to top. Steps six and seven combined create a design called a *chevron*.

8 The raking procedure is repeated, this time moving first from left to right, and then again from right to left.

9 Remember to raise and reposition the rake as described in step seven before completing the second half of the pass each time.

10 One last time, the raking movement is done from top to bottom and bottom to top.

11 Each time, the teeth of the rake are repositioned to straddle the spot where they previously combed.

12 A new tool, called a *comb*, is now passed through the get-gel. Crandall uses a comb she constructed herself out of two narrow strips of wood in which thin "teeth" made from piano wire are sandwiched and spaced approximately 1/8-inch apart. The comb is dragged over the get-gel from top to bottom, creating a combed pattern called a "non-pareil." The non-pareil is a very traditional peacock pattern that everyone associates with marbling.

13 Crandall uses another homemade tool called a bouquet comb. It is similar to the comb above but has two rows of staggered teeth. The bouquet comb is moved over the vat in a serpentine, zigzag motion, producing fine little feathered swirls.

14 Unless you are using a very small piece of fabric (napkin or handkerchief size), you will need an extra set of hands for this next step. Standing at opposite ends of the tank, you and a partner must each hold onto two corners of your fabric. Carefully position it over the tank and lower it slowly. The middle should touch down first, then the rest.

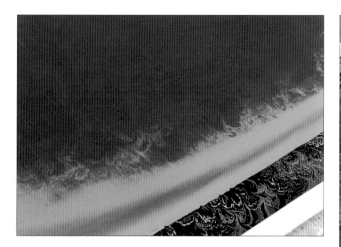

Tip:

After you have done your first marbling, you can re-use the carrageenan as long as there is enough. You must clean it, however. To do this, lay a sheet of newsprint on the surface of the tank to pick up excess dust and paint left over from prior work. Then, skim the surface with a flat board to even the surface tension. Now it is ready for you to apply more paint.

15 The fabric will begin to darken as the pigment is drawn onto it. If you are using a synthetic fabric, you may need to lightly pat all over the surface to ensure that the pattern is taken up. "For best results, the fabric you use should have a smooth surface," says Crandall. "I use either a crepe or a satin-finish fabric. You can't really marble corduroy or velvet or coarse fabric because the fibers will distort the pattern."

16 The taking up of the pattern onto the fabric is almost immediate; it takes fifteen seconds or so. "The alum creates an instantaneous mordant effect," Crandall explains. "Like the tri-sodium phosphate or soda ash used in dyeing, the alum you washed the fabric with helps bond the paint to the fiber." The fabric is ready to pull up when the entire fabric has darkened to indicate saturation.

17 Holding two corners of the fabric, gently lift it up and out of the get-gel and onto a dowel or drying rack, and gently spray with a hose. "Some people just take the fabric and swirl it in a bucket," Crandall says. "This is fine unless you are using a large piece of fabric." The paint will be wet but the pattern will stay in position. After it is dry you won't even be able to scrape it off. Hang the fabric on a line until dry.

The final step—curing—depends upon the type of paint or pigment you used for your marbling. "Sometimes it's best to let acrylic paints cure for a few days," Crandall says. After curing, the paint will need to be heat set. To do this, you can either iron on the reverse side of the fabric with a hot setting, or put it into a commercial clothes dryer for twenty minutes. Then wash in mild soap; soften if desired, hang up to dry again, and iron one last time.

P.B. Schad
Over-marbling with zig-zag pattern

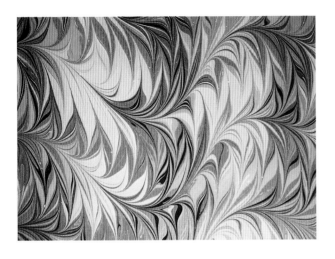

P.B. SCHAD
Over-marbling with zig-zag pattern

LAURA CRANDALL
Marbled silk

P.B. SCHAD
Double marble with fish stencil resist

LAURA CRANDALL
Marbled silk yardage

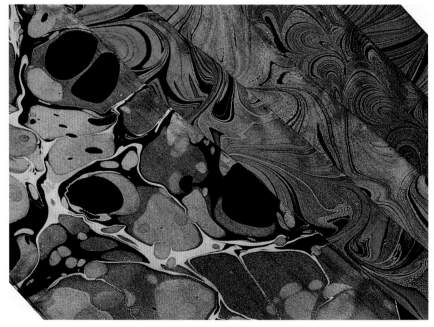

LAURA CRANDALL
Assorted men's ties, marbled silk

P.B. Schad
Silk scarves with over-marbling

P.B. Schad
Men's silk ties, assorted marbling patterns

LYNN CALDWELL
45" x 72" Hand-marbled silk ruana

LYNN CALDWELL
45" x 72" Hand-marbled silk ruana

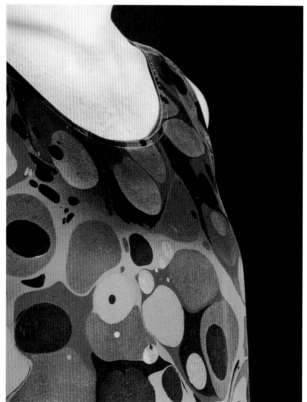

LAURA CRANDALL
Silk charmeuse tank top

LYNN CALDWELL
Hand-marbled silk tie and brace set

LYNN CALDWELL
45" x 72" Hand-marbled silk ruana

CHAPTER 8

Color Theory & Dye Mixology

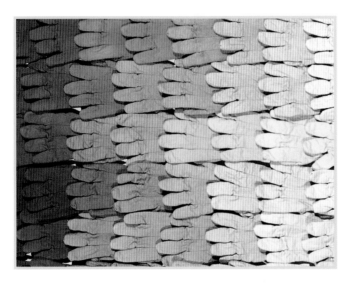

ANNE McKENZIE NICKOLSON
Handscape I, *Controlled Procion®*
vat dyeing on cotton work gloves.

Ever since the year 1666, when Sir Isaac Newton first defined colors in terms of individual wavelengths of light, numerous methods have been devised to categorize and classify the subtleties of the spectrum. Unfortunately, because color perception is such a subjective matter, many different words—value, shade, tint, chroma, brightness, lightness, saturation, brilliance, depth—are used differently to describe three very fundamental attributes of color: what its name is, how pure it is, and how light or dark it is.

Many excellent books on the broader and more complex aspects of color theory are available, and we suggest that you add them to your reference library if you plan to do a lot of dyeing. What follows here is a very general explanation of subtractive color theory specifically as it relates to dyeing fabrics.

What is its Name?

When you ask the question, "What *color* is it?" you are asking what the *hue* is. In its strictest sense, hue is synonymous with the word color.

When the three *primary hues*—red, yellow, blue—are combined, the result is black (or close to it). The combination of any *two* primary hues produces *secondary* colors, or hues:

• Red plus blue produces the hue violet.
• Blue plus yellow produces the hue green.
• Yellow plus red produces the hue orange.

These six hues—red, blue, and yellow (the primary hues) plus purple, green, and orange (the secondary hues)—are often grouped together under the collective category, "cardinal hues."

Tertiary hues are the result of a marriage between a secondary hue—green, for example—and another primary—blue, for example. Blue-green, yellow-orange, blue-violet, and so forth are considered tertiary hues.

When purchasing dyes, you will find that manufacturers often have their own names for colors: one brand's "lemon yellow" is another brand's "bright yellow." However, industry standards require that all colors of a given value must be numbered using a standardized color index system. This ensures that regardless of brand, all dyes with a particular color index number will be essentially the same.

How Dark is it?

The attribute known as *value* describes how light or dark a color/hue is relative to black (on the dark side) and white (on the light side). Gray, for example, is a lighter value of black. Pink is a lighter value of red. Value is sometimes referred to in dye recipes as "depth of shade."

To make a color's value lighter, you use less dye relative to the amount of water called for in the recipe. This creates a tinted, or pastel hue. In general, each time you want to lighten the value by a step, halve the amount of dye required for a fully saturated color.

Because dye powders and solutions vary in strength, the amount needed to achieve the maximum depth of shade varies from color to color. For example, to achieve hues of similar visual saturation (hues that look the same depth to the naked eye), you need almost twice as much yellow dye as you do red.

There is a point at which adding more powder or solution to the water will not enhance its value any further. In fact, too much dye may cause the color to look "off"—for example, some yellows may turn orangey—and the excess will simply wash out during your rinse cycle.

How Pure is it?

In color theory, the term *saturation* refers to the clarity of a color; not its darkness. When you describe a color by using adjectives such as "drab," "dull," "bright," or "clear," you are talking about the color's saturation. It is easiest to think about saturation in terms of two colors of the same value. Pink, for example, has a light *value*. However, two pinks of the same value—say, a clear carnation pink and a light dusty rose—have different levels of saturation.

If you mix additional colors or hues with a saturated color, the color begins to lose its brilliance and is said to be *shaded*. The addition of a small amount of black will impart a grayish shade to the color; the addition of a bit of brown will give any true color an earthy shade. Either of these two colors can be used to create that "dusty pink" described above.

The addition of a color's complement—the color directly opposite it on the color wheel—will also change the shade, or saturation, of a color. As you vary the amount of complementary color mixed with a true color, you will get an increasingly complex range of neutral shades.

Putting it all Together

Most of us were introduced to the principals of color theory as children. We learned that green would magically emerge if we smeared yellow and blue finger paint together. We also learned that while some color combinations yielded delightfully pleasing results, the by-product of other combinations could be downright disgusting.

What is true for finger paints is equally true for dyes. It only takes a pinch of this and a pinch of that to get satisfactory results. But pinch the wrong colors and you are likely to end up with shades that nature never intended the human eye to see!

Although hundreds of custom-mixed colors are available from many dye suppliers, most of these same hues can be created by you in your studio from a small range of basic dyes. Mastering the art of mixing gives you the opportunity to flex your creative muscle and have greater control over not only the product but the process as well.

COLOR CHART

Chart:

The chart to the right shows 21 different dye combinations that will produce 21 different colors from just three basic ones: a yellow, a blue, and a red. (For example, combination #2—8 parts of yellow with 2 parts of red—will produce a sunny yellowish orange; combination #11—8 parts red with 2 parts yellow—will produce a rich reddish orange.) Each block indicates how many parts of each color are called for. The "parts" referred to can be of your choosing: teaspoons, grams, or drops. Just remember to keep the measurement constant throughout, and base it upon the weight of fabric you plan to dye, and the appropriate liquor ratio.

Basic Colors

Y=Yellow

R=Red

B=Blue

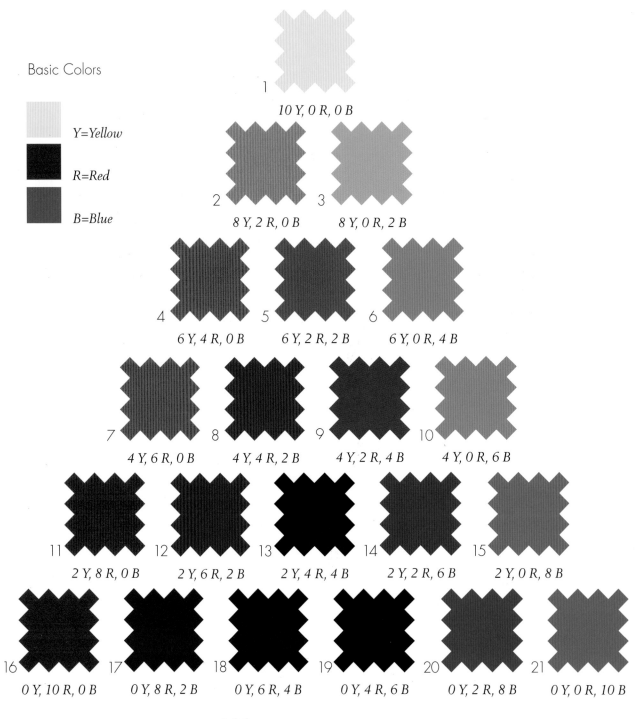

1
10 Y, 0 R, 0 B

2
8 Y, 2 R, 0 B

3
8 Y, 0 R, 2 B

4
6 Y, 4 R, 0 B

5
6 Y, 2 R, 2 B

6
6 Y, 0 R, 4 B

7
4 Y, 6 R, 0 B

8
4 Y, 4 R, 2 B

9
4 Y, 2 R, 4 B

10
4 Y, 0 R, 6 B

11
2 Y, 8 R, 0 B

12
2 Y, 6 R, 2 B

13
2 Y, 4 R, 4 B

14
2 Y, 2 R, 6 B

15
2 Y, 0 R, 8 B

16
0 Y, 10 R, 0 B

17
0 Y, 8 R, 2 B

18
0 Y, 6 R, 4 B

19
0 Y, 4 R, 6 B

20
0 Y, 2 R, 8 B

21
0 Y, 0 R, 10 B

Professional-quality dyes are accompanied by instructions that look like a page out of a chemist's notebook. If you are using powdered fiber-reactive dye, the accompanying recipe may look something like this:

Manufacturer's Recipe

W.O.G. (weight of goods).......1 pound

L:R (liquor ratio)...........................30:1

Dye....................................4% OWG

Salt....................................... 200%

Activator....................................10%

Synthrapol®.............................. 0.2%

Looks vague, doesn't it? Why aren't actual measurements given? The reason is simple: The manufacturer doesn't know what kind of fabric you will be dyeing or how much. By listing all quantities as percentages rather than specific measurements, the relationship between ingredients will always remain constant no matter what the scope of your dyeing project.

As we said in Chapter 3, dye recipes are based on the *weight* of the fabric you are dyeing, not the linear measure. Therefore, weight is the constant variable in each of the percentages given above. To make the recipe useable, you need to translate each of the percentages above into the equivalent weight needed for your specific dyeing project.

Instructions for use vary from supplier to supplier. If you shop around and purchase dye from a variety of sources, you may be confused by the variations in directions. For the sake of simplicity, we suggest that you standardize every recipe provided by your suppliers. To do this, create a table like the one below on a large index card and make a separate card for each dye color you use. Fill out the left column of the card in the order you see here (no matter what order the supplier uses), and then fill in the appropriate percentages specified in the recipe. For example:

Your Recipe Card

Dye name, #, and source	Proportion	Quantity
1. Weight of Goods	1 pound	
2. Liquor Ratio	30:1	
3. Dye	4%	
4. Salt	200%	
5. Activator	10%	
6. *Synthrapol*®	0.2%	

*A table of equivalents for metric and English weights/measures is provided on page 131.

HOW TO READ A RECIPE

Now let's review the recipe step-by-step:

By looking at entry #1, you can see that the recipe is based on the assumption you are going to dye one *pound* of fabric (approximately three t-shirts OR one sweatshirt OR three yards broadcloth). If you want to dye a larger quantity of fabric—say, three pounds instead of one—simply do the math as outlined below, and then multiply the answers to one through five by three.

1. Calculate the liquor ratio (L:R): Typically, the recommended amount of water for full depth of shade is 20 to 40 parts of water to 1 part of dye. (20:1 is usually suggested when hanks of yarn are being dyed; 30:1 or 40:1 are advised when dyeing fabric.)

Here, the recipe calls for a 30:1 liquor ratio. Since we are dyeing 1 pound of fabric, we need 30 x 1 pound of water:

30 pounds H$_2$O = 30 pints = 3 gallons, 3 quarts

2. Calculate the amount of dye powder needed: The amount of dye called for is 4% OWG (4% of the weight of goods). To find out how much dye to use, you must multiply the number of pounds of fabric/fiber you are dyeing by 4%.

To do this, convert the percentage to a decimal— .04—and multiply that number by 16 ounces.

(When working with fractions of a pound—e.g., decimal fragments .99 and smaller—it is usually easier to work with ounces rather than pounds.)

.04 x 16 ounces (the number of ounces in a pound) = .64 ounces of dye needed.

Remember to *weigh* your dye powder, rather than measure it! (Note: 4% is usually the proportion of reactive dye called for to achieve total depth of shade of a given color with a L:R of 30:1. Full depth of shade with an acid dye is usually achived with 1%. Blacks and very dark colors usually require twice that amount.)

3. Calculate the amount of salt needed: Convert the percentage to a decimal: 200% = 2.00. Multiply this number by one pound.

2.00 x 1 pound = 2 pounds of salt needed

4. Calculate the amount of activator needed: Convert the percentage to a decimal: 10% = .10. Multiply this number by 16 ounces.

.10 x 16 ounces = 1.6 ounces of activator needed

5. Calculate the amount of Synthrapol® needed: Convert the percentage (0.2%) to a decimal: 0.2% = .002. Multiply this number by 16 ounces:

.002 x 16 ounces = .03 ounces of *Synthrapol®* needed

Write the measurements computed in each of the steps in the blank spaces on your card. It should look like this:

Your Recipe Card (completed)

Dye name, #, and source	Proportion	Quantity	
1. Weight of Goods	1 pound	1 pound	454 grams
2. Liquor Ratio	30:1	3 gal. 3 qt.	13.6 grams
3. Dye	4%	.64 oz. (9 tsp.)	18.2 grams
4. Salt	200%	2 pounds	908 grams
5. Activator	10%	1.6 oz.	45.4 grams
6. *Synthrapol®*	.2%	.03 oz.	0.91 ml.

Once you have your recipe card completed, you can proceed with the dyeing instructions provided by the manufacturer. Remember, the ingredients and proportions called for will vary depending on the brand you are using, the type of dye you are using (direct, acid, reactive), and whether you are using immersion or direct-application methods. The method for calculating the amounts, however, will remain the same.

Weights & Measures

AVDP (England)	Dry	Liquid
1 teaspoon (tsp)	2.5 grams	5 ml
1 tablespoon (T) = 3 tsp	7.5 grams	15 ml
1 cup = 8 ounces (oz) = 16 T = 48 tsp		236 ml
1/4 cup = 2 oz = 4 T = 12 tsp	30 grams	60 ml
1/2 cup = 4 oz = 8 T = 24 tsp	60 grams	120 ml
3/4 cup = 6 oz = 12 T = 36 tsp	90 grams	180 ml
1 pint = 2 cups = 16 oz		473 ml
1 quart (qt) = 4 cups (c) = 32 oz		95 ml (.95 l)
1.06 quarts		1 liter
1 gallon = 4 qts = 128 oz		3784 ml
1 ounce	28.5 grams	30 ml
1 pound = 16 oz	454 grams	
2.2 pounds	1000 grams = 1 kilogram	

Some Commonly Asked Questions about Acid & Reactive Dyes

Q: What happens if you use a "protein" dye on a cellulosic fiber?

A: Cellulosics have a low tolerance for the lengthy exposure to high heat and the acidic medium that must be used for acid dyes. The two collectively will weaken the fibers.

Q: Since you can use a fiber-reactive dye on silk, why can't you use it on wool?

A: Although under a microscope the cell structure of silk and wool are similar, the size of each wool cell is much larger. For some reason, this prevents fiber-reactive dyes from working their way into the wool. Some color will take, although the shades on wool will be paler than on cellulosics and silk, and will be slightly heathered. Of course, you may like this effect, so try it and see! On the other hand, since acid dyes are less expensive and require fewer additives, you may lose more than you gain by putting a fiber-reactive on wool.

Q: Direct dyes don't seem to care which fiber you use. So why deal with acid or fiber-reactives in the first place?

A: You lose something for the sake of the convenience. With direct dyes, you lose brilliance and wash-fastness. For home use—e.g., giving a new splash of color to faded sheets or sneakers—this may not matter. But for works of art or any project that will be subjected to repeated washings or exposure to strong light, acid or fiber-reactive dyes are the way to go.

How to mix dye into a stock solution

Some dye jobs involve small amounts of fabric, and the fractional amounts of dye often called for can be hard to measure in the powdered state. For this reason, many suppliers suggest that a liquid solution be mixed up in advance and used instead of dry powder. A 1% solution is the most convenient measure for most purposes.

1% Solution

To Make:	Dye	Water
1 cup of 1% dye solution	1 tsp/ 2.5 grams	1 cup/ 250 ml
1 quart of solution	4 tsp/ 10 grams	1 quart/ 1 liter

Note: These measurements are approximate, and vary according to the density of the dye powder being used.

United States

ATELIER DE PARIS
1556 South Fairfax Avenue
Los Angeles, California 90019
310-553-6636
H. DuPont dyes

BROOKS AND FLYNN
PO Box 2639
Rohnert Park, California 94927-2639
800-822-2372
Everything possible for fiber artists: dyes, fabric, tools.

COLART AMERICAS INC.
11 Constitution Avenue
Piscataway, New Jersey 08855-1396
908-562-0770
908-562-0941
Artists' materials for dyeing and painting, including Deka.

CREATEX
14 Airport Park Road
East Granby, Connecticut 02626
800-243-2712
203-653-0643
Dyes and artists' supplies.

DECORATIVE PAPERS
PO Box 749
Easthampton, Massachusetts 01027
Acrylic marbling supplies.

DEKA
Decart Inc.
PO Box 309
Morrisville, Vermont 05661
802-888-4217
802-888-4123 fax
Manufacturer of DEKA dyes, paints, and crafts accessories.

DHARMA TRADING COMPANY
1604 Fourth Street
San Rafael, California 94915
415-456-1211
800-542-5227
Major supplier of textiles and blank items (infant clothing, sweatshirts, pants, etc.); weaving supplies; yarns; silk painting supplies (paints, dyes, and fabric); Procion fiber-reactive liquid and powdered; Dupont, Jacquard (dyes and paints), blank silk earrings; books.

EARTH GUILD
33 Haywood Street
Asheville, North Carolina 28801
704-255-7818
800-327-8448
Tools and materials for all sorts of handcrafts. Synthetic and natural dyestuffs, books, tools.

ORIENTAL SILK COMPANY
8377 Beverly Boulevard
Los Angeles, California 90048
213-651-2323
213-651-2323 fax
Mail order and shop; fine imported silks, woolens, porcelains, hand embroideries, and linens from China and the Orient.

PRO-CHEMICAL & DYE, INC.
PO Box 14
Somerset, Massachusetts 02726
508-676-3838
508-676-3980 fax
One of the most exhaustive sources of dyes, paints, tools, and training for textile artists in the East. Procion H, MX; Sabracon, Sabraset, Diazol, Indigo, Pebeo, myriad resists, pre-measured kits and more.

QUALIN INTERNATIONAL
PO Box 31145
San Francisco, California 94131
415-333-8500
Superb source of artist-ready silk.

RUPERT, GIBBON & SPIDER
PO Box 425
Healdsburg, California 95448
800-442-0455
Manufacturer of Jacquard paints and dyes for textiles; books, accessories, textile arts supplies, fabric. Some mail order as well as referrals to retail outlets.

CARTER SMITH
25 Pleasant Street
Nahant, Massachusetts 01908
617-581-9706
Bulk stock of sodium hypochlorite for stripping/discharging.

SUREWAY TRADING ENTERPRISES
826 Pine Avenue, Suite 5 & 6
Niagara Falls, New York 14301
716-282-4887
716-282-8211 fax
Silk fabric, threads, scarves and ties, H. Dupont and Sennelier dyes; gutta and other silk painting accessories.

THAI SILKS
252 State Street
Los Altos, California 95125
415-948-8611
415-948-3426 fax
One of the largest distributors of natural silk yardage in the U.S..

HAND-MARBLED PAPERS
PO Box 78
Spring Mills, Pennsylvania 16875
814-422-8651
Marbling supplies.

Canada

EHB DESIGNS
132 Rosedale Valley Road
Toronto, Ontario M4W 1P7
416-964-0634
Procion and Sumifix dyes and all the auxiliary chemicals; high lustre silk yarn, merino 2/6 yarn; superb instruction and customer support.

EUROPEAN TEXTILES
432 Queen Street West
Toronto, Ontario M5A 1T4
416-366-3332
Silks and fabrics.

G & S DYE & ACCESSORIES LTD.
300 Steelcase Road West #19
Markham, Ontario L3R 2W2
905-415-8559; 416-596-0550
416-596-0493 fax
Over eight brands of dyes and paints and auxiliary supplies. Full range of silk fabric and scarves in over 80 different combinations of weights and sizes.

Germany

C. KREUL GMBH
Hainbrunnenstrasse 8
Forcheim D-91301
0 9191-614-0
0 9191-61412 and 6 14 53 fax
Javana and Goya paints and dyes, tools and instruction manuals for textile painting and design.

UHLIG GMBH
Horst-Uhlig-Str. 3
Laudert 56291
0 67 46 / 8 01-0
0 67 46 / 8 01 90 fax
Manufacturer of steam- and iron-fixed paints, gutta pens, painting tables, and fittings for silk painting.

Great Britain

COLART FINE ART & GRAPHICS
Whitefriars Avenue
Harrow, Middlesex HA3 5RH
081-427-4343
081-863-7177 fax
Artists' materials for dyeing and painting, including Deka.

FRED ALDOUS LTD.
PO Box 135, 37 Lever Street
Manchester, M60 1UX
0161-236-2477
0161-236-6075 fax
Mail order and shop; full range of craft materials including materials for dyeing, batik work, silk painting, fabric painting, etc.

KEMTEX SERVICES LTD.
Tameside Business Centre, Windmill Lane
Denton, Manchester M34 3QS
0161 320 6505
0161 335 9101 fax
Textile consultants, reactive and acid dyestuffs, paints, tools, booklets, and chemicals; Kemtex craft dyes.

PURE SILK
Old Church Room
Hill Row
Haddenham, Cambridgeshire CB6 3TL
01353-741538
White scarves for painters; painted scarves and ties. Mail order, shop, manufacturer.

GEORGE WEIL & SONS LTD.
The Warehouse, 20 Reading Arch Road
Redhill, Surrey RH1 1H9
01737-778868
01737-778894 fax
Extensive mail order resource for all textile arts supplies. UK agent for Deka, Javana, Kreul; also Dupont, Hunt Speedball, Delta paints and dyestuffs; screen printing, silk painting, and batik supplies.

GEORGE WEIL & SONS LTD.
18 Hanson Street
London W1P 7DB
0171-580-3763.
Retail shop. See description above.

France

H. DUPONT
86 Rue de Clery
Paris F-75002
33 1 42.33.84.71
33 1 43.54.61.69 fax
Shop and showroom for all H. Dupont textile arts products, including acid dyes, gutta, thinners, fabric paints, equipment, and tools.

LE PRINCE DE PARIS
19 Rue de Clery
Paris 75002
1 42.36.59.10
1 40.26.34.78 fax
Manufacturer of LePrince textile paints.

Australia

BATIK OETORO PTY LTD.
203 Avoca Street
Randwick 2031
02 398-6201
02 398-1173 fax
Manufacturer, wholesale, and mail order. Batik waxes and canting tools, fabric paints and dyes (Derimarine K, Drimalan-F, Procion MX, Naphthol, direct, acid, and synthetic indigo); books, tools, and auxiliaries.

Professional Organizations & Resources

United States

AMERICAN CRAFTS COUNCIL
72 Spring Street, New York, New York
212-274-0630

SURFACE DESIGN ASSOCIATION
PO Box 20799, Oakland, California
510-841-2008

THE TEXTILE MUSEUM
2320 S Street, NW, Washington, D.C.
202-232-7223

Canada

THE MUSEUM FOR TEXTILES
55 Centre Avenue, Toronto, Ontario
416-599-5321

ONTARIO CRAFTS COUNCIL
Chalmers Building, Ontario, Canada
416-977-3551

TEXTILE DYERS AND PRINTERS ASSOCIATION
PO Box 6828, Station A, Toronto, Ontario

Europe

ASSOCIATION NATIONALE POUR LA PROMOTION DES ARTS DECORATIFS SUR TISSUS
17 Rue de Clery, Paris, France
42.36.59.10

THE GUILD OF SILK PAINTERS
The Old Brewery, Brewery Yard, High Street
Hastings, England

Arts & Crafts Centers/ Non-Degree Programs, Professional Enrichment

ARROWMONT SCHOOL OF ARTS AND CRAFTS
PO Box 567, 556 Parkway
Gatlinburg, Tennessee 37738-0567
615-436-5860; fax 615-430-4101
One of the nation's most prestigious visual arts centers. Year-round courses for all levels, including children, conferences. Over 150 visiting faculty teach courses in fiber, fabric, painting, papermaking, and more.

DORLAND MOUNTAIN ARTS COLONY
PO Box 6, Temecula, California 92593
909-676-5039

HAYSTACK MOUNTAIN SCHOOL OF CRAFTS
Deer Isle, Maine 04627
207-348-2306
Prestigious summer arts school featuring workshops, open studios, lectures, presentations by internationally known faculty artists.

PENLAND SCHOOL OF CRAFTS
Penland Road, Penland, North Carolina 28765
704-765-2359
All sorts of courses in artisanry.

PETER'S VALLEY CRAFT CENTER
Route 615, 19 Kuhn Road, Layton, New Jersey 07851
201-948-5200
Established in 1970. Non-profit organization to provide opportunities for the development of craft skills. Nationally known artist/teachers. Summer workshops, classes for children, annual craft fair, artists' residencies, demonstrations, exhibitions, etc.

College Degree Programs in Textiles

California

ACADEMY OF ART COLLEGE
79 New Montgomery Street
San Francisco, California 94105-3410
415-274-2266; 800-544-ARTS

CALIFORNIA COLLEGE OF ARTS & CRAFTS
5212 Broadway at College Ave, Oakland, California 94618
510-653-8118

CALIFORNIA STATE UNIVERSITY / LONG BEACH
Long Beach, California 90032-4221
213-343-2752

CALIFORNIA STATE UNIVERSITY/NORTHRIDGE
18111 Nordhoff Street, Northridge, California 91330-0001
818-885-3777

UNIVERSITY OF CALIFORNIA/DAVIS
Davis, California 95616-2971
916-752-29771

Georgia

GEORGIA INSTITUTE OF TECHNOLOGY
Atlanta, Georgia 30332
404-894-2000

SAVANNAH COLLEGE OF ART AND DESIGN
PO Box 3146, Savannah, Georgia 31402-3146
912-238-2483

Illinois

NORTHERN ILLINOIS UNIVERSITY
DeKalb, Illinois 60115-2864
815-753-0446

SCHOOL OF THE ART INSTITUTE OF CHICAGO
37 South Wabash, Chicago, Illinois 60603-3103
312-899-1295; 800-232-SAIC

Kansas

KANSAS STATE UNIVERSITY
112 Anderson Hall, Manhattan, Kansas 66506
913-532-6250; 800-432-8270

UNIVERSITY OF KANSAS
126 Strong Hall, Lawrence, Kansas 66045-1910
913-864-3911

Maryland

MARYLAND INSTITUTE, COLLEGE OF ART
1300 Mount Royal Avenue
Baltimore, Maryland 21217-4192
410-225-2294

UNIVERSITY OF MARYLAND/COLLEGE PARK
College Park, Maryland 20742-5235
301-314-8385

Massachusetts

UNIVERSITY OF MASSACHUSETTS/DARTMOUTH
Old Westport Road
North Dartmouth, Massachusetts 02747
508-999-8000
The only comprehensive textile program in the northeast.

Michigan

CENTER FOR CREATIVE STUDIES, COLLEGE OF ART & DESIGN
245 East Kirby, Detroit, Michigan 48202-4034
313-872-3118
One of the 7 largest undergrad professional art colleges in the U.S.; 17 concentrations in the fine arts & design fields.

NORTHERN MICHIGAN UNIVERSITY
Marquette, Michigan 49855
906-227-2650; 800-689-9797

UNIVERSITY OF MICHIGAN/ANN ARBOR
Ann Arbor, Michigan 48109-1316
313-764-7433

Missouri

KANSAS CITY ART INSTITUTE
4415 Warwick Boulevard, Kansas City, Missouri 64111
816-561-4852

NORTHWEST MISSOURI STATE UNIVERSITY
Maryville, Missouri 64468-6001
816-562-1562; 800-633-1175

New York

CORNELL UNIVERSITY
410 Thurston Avenue, Ithaca, New York 14853-2488
607-255-2000

FASHION INSTITUTE OF TECHNOLOGY/SUNY
7th Avenue at 27th Street
New York City, New York 10001-5992
212-760-7675

PARSONS SCHOOL OF DESIGN, NEW SCHOOL FOR
SOCIAL RESEARCH
66 Fifth Avenue, New York City, New York 10011-8878
212-229-8910; 800-252-0852

PRATT INSTITUTE
200 Willoughby Avenue, Brooklyn, New York 11205
718-636-3600

ROCHESTER INSTITUTE OF TECHNOLOGY SCHOOL
FOR AMERICAN CRAFTS
One Lomb Drive, Rochester, New York 14623-5604
716-475-6631

North Carolina

NORTH CAROLINA STATE UNIVERSITY
Raleigh, North Carolina 27695
919-737-2434

Ohio

BOWLING GREEN STATE UNIVERSITY
Bowling Green, Ohio 43403
419-372-2086

CLEVELAND INSTITUTE OF ART
11141 East Boulevard, Cleveland, Ohio 44106-1700
216-421-7418; 800-223-6500 in state;
800-223-4700 out of state

KENT STATE UNIVERSITY
Kent, Ohio 44242-0001
216-672-2444

Oregon

PACIFIC NORTHWEST COLLEGE OF ART
1219 Southwest Park Avenue
Portland, Oregon 97205-2430
503-226-0462

Pennsylvania

EDINBORO UNIVERSITY OF PENNSYLVANIA
Edinboro, Pennsylvania 16444
814-732-2000; 800-626-2203

TYLER SCHOOL OF ART OF TEMPLE UNIVERSITY
Beech & Penrose Avenue, Elkins Park, Pennsylvania 19126
215-782-2828

MOORE COLLEGE OF ART & DESIGN
20th and the Parkway, Philadelphia, Pennsylvania 19103
215-568-4515; 800-523-2025

PHILADELPHIA COLLEGE OF TEXTILES AND SCIENCE
School House Lane & Henry Avenue
Philadelphia, Pennsylvania 19144
215-951-2800

UNIVERSITY OF THE ARTS
Broad & Pine Streets, Philadelphia, Pennsylvania 19102
215-875-4808

CARNEGIE MELLON UNIVERSITY
Pittsburgh, Pennsylvania 15213-3891
412-268-2082

ALBRIGHT COLLEGE
PO Box 15234, Reading, Pennsylvania 19612
215-921-7512; 800-252-1856

Rhode Island

RHODE ISLAND SCHOOL OF DESIGN
2 College Street, Providence, Rhode Island 02903-2784
401-454-6300

Tennessee

MEMPHIS COLLEGE OF ART
Overton Park, 1930 Poplar Avenue
Memphis, Tennessee 38104-2764
901-726-4085; 800-727-1088

MIDDLE TENNESSEE STATE UNIVERSITY
Murfreesboro, Tennessee 37132
615-898-2111

Virginia

VIRGINIA INSTITUTE OF TECHNOLOGY
Box 391, Charlottesville, Virginia 22902
804-296-5511

Wisconsin

UNIVERSITY OF WISCONSIN / MILWAUKEE
PO Box 413, Milwaukee, Wisconsin 53201-0413
414-229-6164

Canada

NOVA SCOTIA COLLEGE OF ART & DESIGN
5163 Duke Street, Halifax, Nova Scotia, BB3J 3J6
902-422-7381

BRESCIA COLLEGE
1285 Western Road, London, Ontario, N6G1H2
519-432-8353

CAPILANO COLLEGE
2055 Purcell Way, North Vancouver
British Columbia 7J3H5
604-986-1911

CONCORDIA UNIVERSITY
1455 de Maisonneuve Blvd West
Montreal, Quebec, H3G1M8
514-848-2424

APPENDIX D: DIRECTORY OF ARTISTS

JEANNE ADAMS
945 North 5th Street
Philadelphia, PA 19123
215-413-0149

JOSEPH ALMYDA
1100 Bissonnet, Houston, TX 77005
713-522-9116

LORI & MARSHALL BACIGALUPI/
KISS OF THE WOLF
PO Box 1211, 807 S. Ponca Avenue
Norman, OK 73070
405-364-8150; fax 329-8833

JUDITH BIRD
1429 Quincy Street
Port Townsend, WA 98368
360-379-8330

AMY BLACKSTONE
1836 Bainbridge Street
Philadelphia, PA 19146
215-732-2181

DOROTHY CALDWELL
RR1, Hastings, Ontario K0L 1YO, Canada
705-696-2092

LYNN CALDWELL
927 Britta Lane, Batavia, IL 60510
708-406-1495

LUCINDA CATHCART/CHAMELEON
22 Liberty Street, Newburyport, MA 01950
508-463-7623

JUDITH CONTENT
827 Matadero Avenue, Palo Alto, CA 94306
415-857-0289

LAURA CRANDALL
113 West 4th Street, Bloomington, IN 47402
812-331-7257

NANETTE DAVIS-SHAKLHO
1289 E. Grand Avenue #318
Escondido, CA 92027
619-745-6091; 788-7860

ASTRITH DEYRUP
395 Riverside Drive, New York, NY 10025
212-749-6258

ARNELLE DOW
448 Milton Street, Cincinnati, OH 45210
513-421-9549

NOEL DYRENFORTH
11 Shepherds Hill, London, England N65QJ
0181 348-0956; fax 0181 348-0956

MICHAEL DAVIS & LAURIE GUNDERSON/
GUNDERSON-DAVIS
171 1/2 High Street, Elkins, WV 26241
304-636-1557

DAVID & LINDA FRANCE HARTGE/
KALEIDOSILK
140 Haviland Mill Road
Brookeville, MD 20833
301-774-2671

ANA LISA HEDSTROM
1420 45th Street, Emeryville, CA 94608
415-949-2861 h/studio

KYMBERLY HENSON
30 East 5th Street
Newport, KY 41071
606-431-3840

VIGGO HOLM MADSEN
5 Meldon Avenue, Albertson, NY 11507
516-741-5952

MICHELLE MARCUSE
1400 North 4th Street
Philadelphia, PA 19122
215-235-3483

ANNE MCKENZIE NICHOLSON
5020 North Illinois Street
Indianapolis, IN 46208
317-257-8929

MARIANNA HAMILTON ROSS
505 Greely Street, Orlando, FL 32804
407-843-7015

BILLI R.S. ROTHOVE/
GALLERY COORDINATOR
ARROWMONT SCHOOL OF ARTS AND CRAFTS
556 Parkway, Gatlinburg, TN 37738
615-436-5860

PEGGY RUSSELL/IRO DESIGN
450 Harrison Avenue, Boston, MA 02118
617-426-3850

P.B. SCHAD
Box 234, Huntvale, PA 19006
215-659-5428

CARTER SMITH
25 Pleasant Street, Nahant, MA 01908
617-581-9706

141

GLOSSARY

ACETIC ACID 56%
A concentrated liquid acid eleven times stronger than household vinegar. Used in dyeing wool, silk, nylon and polyester.

ACID DYE
A dyestuff made from the salts of organic acids; used primarily on protein fibers such as wool and silk.

ACTIVATOR
An alkaline substance such as soda ash or tri-sodium phosphate, added to a fiber-reactive dyebath to keep the dye in the desired pH range of 10 to 10.5

ALGINATE
A seaweed derivative used as an anti-migrant. High-viscosity alginates are recommended for cotton; low-viscosity alginates are recommended for screen printing on silk or synthetic fibers.

ALKALI
A substance with a basic, rather than acidic, pH level. Generally a soluble salt consisting largely of potassium carbonate or sodium carbonate. (See activator, above)

ALUM
Any one of several aluminum sulfate compounds often used as a mordant when marbling.

AMMONIUM SULFATE
A salt that improves the leveling and exhausting of color when using acid dyes. Replaces acetic or citric acids when dyeing with wash-fast acid dyes.

ANTI-MIGRANT
A substance added to a dye to slow down its ability to spread or bleed into a fabric once it is applied. Most traditional anti-migrants are cellulose derivatives. (Alginates are not cellulose derivatives)

ANTI-SPREAD
A transparent liquid that is painted over an entire area of fabric prior to dyeing to cut down the absorbency of the fibers, thereby preventing the dye from spreading.

BATIK WAX
Blend of 25% microcrystalline and 75% paraffin waxes. Melting point 150°F.

BEESWAX
A natural source of wax used as a resist in batik dyeing. Melting point of 130°F.

CARRAGEENAN
A natural thickener used as a suspending agent; it is added to water to create a medium on which marbling pigments can be suspended. (See methyl cellulose)

CELLULOSE/CELLULOSIC FIBER
A fiber derived from some plant form and which shares a common molecular structure: cotton, linen, rayon, hemp.

CHEMICAL WATER
A blend of water, urea, Synthrapol® and sometimes water softener; used with fiber-reactive dyes to create a dye paint.

CITRIC ACID
A substitute for acetic acid 56% and vinegar in acid dye recipes. Citric acid can be substituted for acetic acid in equal measure. Citric acid is often preferred over vinegar and acetic acid because it imparts no sour smell during dyeing.

COLD WAX
A soft, water-soluble waxy resist that can be applied like a paste without being heated and/or melted first.

DIRECT DYE
Sometimes called a hot-water dye. A popular type of dye which can be used in hot tap water; requires no leveling or exhausting agents. Convenient but poor light- and wash-fastness.

DISCHARGE
The process of removing color from a fabric in a controlled manner. Discharge chemicals are usually very caustic and should be used in areas with superb ventilation.

DYE
A water-soluble, transparent coloring agent that saturates a fiber and is absorbed into the fiber.

DYE PAINT
A combination of chemical water (urea, Synthrapol®, alkali), dye concentrate, alginate or paste mix, and water. Used to apply reactive dye directly to fabric in a painterly manner.

EXHAUSTING AGENT
An additive to the dyebath which helps push the dye into the fiber. Usually salt or acid depending on type of dye used.

EXHAUST DYEING
Another term for immersion dyeing. Also called long-liquor ratio dyeing.

FORMUSOL
Brand name for sodium formaldehyde sulfoxylate, a chemical used for very fast stripping and discharging on wool, silk, cotton, and nylon.

GLAUBER'S SALT
Another name for sodium sulfate.

GUTTA
The French word for resist. Also, the liquid resist used to outline designs and block the flow of dye. Usually black or clear. Available in water-based and solvent-based varieties.

FIXING
The process of setting a dye so that it will remain in the fiber. Fixing is achieved in different ways depending on the dye used: Usually by heat, steam, or air-curing.

LEVELING AGENT
An additive to the dye bath which helps slow down the rapid absorption of dye by a fiber, thereby helping minimize streaking and improving even distribution of the color.

LIQUOR RATIO
The measurement of water called for in a dye recipe. Often abbreviated L:R.

LONG-LIQUOR RATIO DYEING
Another term for immersion or exhaust dyeing.

METAPHOS
Brand name for a softener added to water to increase the absorption of the dye.

METHYL CELLULOSE
A cellulose derivative used to thicken water for marbling.

MICROCRYSTALLINE WAX
A petroleum-based synthetic beeswax which produces less crackle than other waxes. Often mixed with paraffin to soften it. Also called sticky wax.

MONAGUM
A modified starch gum which, when mixed with household bleach, can be used for stripping and discharging.

MORDANT
A mineral (usually a metal) added to a natural dye to increase its affinity for the fiber.

PARAFFIN
A petroleum wax used in batik dyeing; tends to be very brittle after it dries on the cloth. When used alone, it tends to sit on the surface of the cloth and can flake off when handled too much.

PIGMENT
An insoluble colored particle that sits on the surface of a material and remains there through the help of bonding agents (alum) or fixing agents (heat).

PRESIST®
Brand name for a water-soluble liquid resist similar to traditional gutta. Tends to work best if used on dry rather than damp fabric.

PROCION®
Brand name for a family of fiber-reactive dyes developed by the Zeneca Corporation (a division of I.C.I.) Procion® MX dyes are highly reactive and can cure at room temperature; Procion® H dye is moderately reactive and is usually set with steam.

GLOSSARY

PROTEIN FIBER
A fiber derived from an animal source and which shares a common molecular structure. Silk and wool.

REACTIVE DYE
A category of dyes that become part of the fiber. Excellent wash-fastness and light-fastness. Generally require an alkaline environment.

RESIST
Any barrier used to block the flow and penetration of a dye. String, clamps, stencils, wax, etc are also resists.

SHORT-LIQUOR RATIO DYEING
Another term for direct-application dye techniques such as spraying or painting.

SIZE
In marbling, the water bath which has been thickened with carrageenan, or methyl cellulose or other substance.

SODA ASH
Another name for sodium carbonate (see below), an activator used with fiber-reactive dyes.

SODIUM ALGINATE
A seaweed thickener used in direct-application painting techniques.

SODIUM BICARBONATE
Baking soda; a small amount is combined with water and dye to create a weak alkali solution that can be used for direct application.

SODIUM CARBONATE
An alkali used with reactive dye in the dyebath to permanently set colors on cellulose. Also called soda ash.

SODIUM HYDROSULFITE
Chemical used for gentle stripping and discharging of color.

SYNTHRAPOL®
Brand name for a very concentrated and gentle liquid detergent that is used to wet out the fiber; also pre-scour and after-wash. Its pH is neutral (pH 7), which makes it appropriate for use with acid and reactive dyes.

TJANTING
A wooden-handled batik tool with a bulbous metal reservoir at the end and a spout that protrudes from the bottom of the reservoir. It is used by dipping the reservoir into melted wax; the spout regulates the flow of wax and enables the user to draw lines that range in thickness from fine to broad.

TJAP
A metal plate carved with an intricate design, used to apply wax to a fabric prior to batik dyeing.

TSP
Tri-sodium phosphate; a strong alkali used as an activator for fiber-reactive dyes.

THIOX
Brand name for thiourea dioxide, a chemical used for fast-color stripping and discharging on cellulose.

UREA
Ammonium carbamate; an additive which increases the solubility of a dye (i.e., helps it remain in thickened state) and acts as a humectant (i.e., keeps the moisture in a dampened fabric long enough to enable the dye to penetrate).

WEAK ACID DYE
Another name for Class III acid dyes, also known as "milling dyes" or "Wash-Fast®" acid dyes.

WEIGHT OF GOODS
A term used to designate the weight of fabric being dyed. Often abbreviated W.O.G.

WETTING OUT
The thorough saturation of a fiber or fabric with water prior to dyeing. Proper wetting out is necessary to ensure even dyeing.